india

a wealth of diversity

Edited by Arif Ali

HANSIB

Published in 1997 by Hansib Publications
Tower House, 141-149 Fonthill Road, London N4 3HF England.

Printed in the United Kingdom by
Caledonian International Book Manufacturing, Glasgow.
Colour Origination by Graphic Ideas Studios, London.
Production by Cut & Paste DTP Services, Welwyn.
Principal Photography by Pankaj Shah.

British Library Cataloguing in Publication Data.
A catalogue record for this book is available from the British Library.

ISBN 1-870518-61-6

COVER PHOTOGRAPHS: Pankaj Shah
INSIDE FRONT COVER: **SIMLA,** *a famous hill station and the capital of Himachal
Pradesh, nestles in the Himalayan foothills at an altitude of over two kilometres. In
1946 the leaders of India's nationalist movement met here at a critical stage in the
struggle for independence. Simla is a popular holiday destination. Photograph by
Amlan Paliwal.*
INSIDE BACK COVER: **SREE PADMABHASWAMY TEMPLE** *in Kerala is a classic
example of Dravidian style.*

Acknowledgements

In *India - A Wealth of Diversity*, we have endeavoured to capture the flavour, spirit and essence of the world's second most populous nation - with its five thousand years of history, culture and civilisation; its great religions; its hundreds of languages; its unparalleled variety in every sphere of the natural world.

Such an endeavour is inevitably a collective one, and I have been fortunate enough to attract an excellent core team to work with me on this project.

I would like to extend special thanks to Paul Fraser, Shareef Ali, Ella Barnes, John Hughes, Isha Persaud, Keith Bennett and Gonaseelan (Robert) Govender. These seven people - either members of my family or close friends - have, in certain cases, worked alongside me for thirty years. Others came back, on assignment, from their other responsibilities, specifically for this book. They all displayed an immense commitment, based on their deep understanding of the ideals and principles which motivated our work. I cannot thank them enough.

To produce a work of this magnitude in the time we had available requires an extraordinary degree of application. This takes a toll on both the individuals concerned and their families. I would, therefore, like to express sympathy, understanding and appreciation to my colleagues' families as well as to my own.

My thanks go also to Sam Rajah, Martin Platt and Bryan Carroll; and to all the hidden and unknown people who have helped and contributed behind the scenes.

Special thanks are due to those who offered unstinting support, but who we have inexcusably overlooked; to those who contributed articles, photographs or ideas, which I decided not to use; to the hundreds of authors, scholars, officials, consultants and social activists, in India, Britain and other countries, whose ideas and publications formed our points of reference for study, stimulation, verification, and cross-checking; and to all those in the High Commission for India, government ministries and agencies, official bodies and the private sector, who have all extended the utmost cooperation and assistance throughout.

May this book prove to be my way of saying thank you. It is dedicated to India and to all people of Indian origin, background and culture, wherever their national home may be. May you continue to enrich the world in the 21st century.

With special appreciation to the High Commissioner for India in the United Kingdom, His Excellency Dr L. M. Singhvi, Baroness Shreela Flather, Zerbanoo Gifford, Piara Singh Khabra MP, Professor Bhikhu Parekh, Lord Swraj Paul and Keith Vaz MP.

Thanks also to Derek Biddle, Susan Cameron, T. Haridas, P. Kapur, Gulam Meeran, Kuttan Menon, G. K. Noon, Anna Maria and Fabio Rossi, Lady Maureen Thomas, Nazmu Virani, Air India, The British Museum, The High Commission for India's Press & Information Department and its Nehru Centre, Mysteries of India Holidays and Small Group Tours (London), Sultan Shahin, Talmaz Ahmed, Ranee Battacharya, R. P. Puri, India International Centre and Central News Agency Pvt Ltd (Delhi), and The Great India Tour Company (Thiruvananthapuram).

Arif Ali
London, July 1997

Foreword

THE PUBLICATION of *India - A Wealth of Diversity* does not result from a whim or a fancy. It is the culmination of years of thought and planning. It realises an aspiration that we have long cherished. One can almost say that it represents a dream come true.

The seventh in Hansib's 'Nation' series, this book is also a first. It is our first title to profile and introduce an Asian country and the first to depict a nation of India's truly stupendous size and scale.

Although many people have welcomed this book's publication and encouraged us in our endeavours, it is in every sense an independent initiative and has been so from the time it was conceived through to publication.

It is a great honour and responsibility to publish this book to coincide with the 50th anniversary of India's independence, an occasion of such momentous significance that we felt obligated to make our own contribution to its celebration.

The independence of India represented not only a new departure in the life of an ancient nation and civilisation, but also the beginning of the end for the great colonial empires. After the jewel was removed from its crown, in less than a generation, the greatest and most powerful empire that history had ever seen had disintegrated, as had its rivals and partners.

Perhaps for this very reason, although there has been no shortage of raj and empire nostalgia, there is still a tendency in the West to downplay and underestimate the significance of this great event. However, when one comes to assess at the lasting influence of those individuals who have shaped and moulded the 20th century, the name of Mahatma Gandhi will surely be placed at the very top by serious and objective historians. How ironic it is, therefore, that Winston Churchill, himself one of the great figures of British history, should have sought to dismiss Gandhi as a "fakir in a loin cloth".

The independence of India was, of course, a moment of great triumph. It was also a time of tragedy and trauma. The horrendous circumstances that accompanied Partition not only took their toll on millions, they left a legacy that sometimes festers to this day. Yet India's thriving secularism, and the recent meticulous efforts to normalise and harmonise relations with all her neighbours, increasingly represent the main trend of developments. From the Balkans to the Americas, there is no shortage of examples of how less pervasive conflicts can seem almost impossible to heal. That India has set such an example of toleration and magnanimity in this regard is but one example of the underlying moral strength that continually reinvigorates the national spirit on the basis of 5,000 and more years of unbroken civilisation.

This book represents a compilation of the thoughts and research of many people. It does not primarily seek to break new ground as such, but rather to present, in an accessible and easy to follow fashion, India's own story, showing the country's achievements and potential, as well as its shortcomings, something from which no country on earth is immune. We have aimed to produce a book in which Indian people can take pride and which can also interest and inspire those who may be considering investing in this vast tiger economy, as well as those whose interest may lie in the country's rich cultural heritage or outstanding scenic beauty.

Editing this book was itself an educational experience for myself and my team. It reminded us of the fact that the Western media, time and again, fails to present India as it deserves to be presented. But we have moved on from the times when it could be considered sufficient to blame them alone. Indian entrepreneurs are renowned for their skills and success around the world. The country's film industry is the greatest in the world, although it is far from reaching its potential in terms of the contribution it could make to a global projection of the nation. It is surely high time for the nation's entrepreneurs to realise that the coming 21st century - just a couple of short years away - will be one dominated and moulded by information technology and the communications industry as never before. As the Jewish diaspora has done so astutely, their Indian counterparts need to look afresh at their business strategy for survival and expansion, exploring, for example, the potential for shareholding in some of the major international media conglomerates. There could hardly be a better and more pressing time, when satellites are encircling the earth and bombarding the people of India with an unprecedented variety of images and influences.

This is something to which no nation or people can remain indifferent with impunity. More than ever before, reality is being shaped to accord with appearance. Within this context, too many people, including some very famous writers of Indian origin, have a tendency to visit India for a few weeks only to portray the country in a negative and harshly critical light, forgetting that fifty years is as momentary as the snap of the fingers in the odyssey of a nation that enjoys, an uninterrupted history of 5,000 years of culture and civilisation. When set against this benchmark, what is really striking is not the scale of the difficulties but rather the extent of the achievements, in every field from politics to economics, and from culture to science and technology. Considering the deep-seated and pervasive nature of the caste system, for example, who would have thought that a man like K.R. Narayanan, a member of a so-called 'lower caste', could be installed in the highest office of state, as President of the Republic, with the support of all the country's major political parties, before the 50th anniversary of independence?

Likewise, what hard-headed trader or investor can realistically afford to ignore the Indian market? Already one of the largest industrial economies, the world's second most populous country is set to see its population pass the billion mark before we enter the new millennium. Its middle class of 300 million exceeds the total population of the European Union, with 50 million of these people - almost equivalent to the total population of the United Kingdom - now enjoying European levels of style and consumption.

Ever since independence dawned half a century ago, nations and peoples around the world have looked up to India. It has been a global force for peace and justice. As the vanguard in the great wave of decolonisation, it helped to fashion the modern Commonwealth and took the lead in the formation of the Non-Aligned Movement, the most representative forum of formerly colonised nations in Asia, Africa, the Caribbean, South America, the South Pacific, and even Europe. For many years, India's relations with the former Soviet Union were a model for states with different social and economic systems. The five principles of peaceful coexistence, which guide India's foreign policy, are a creative adaptation of the country's traditional and time-honoured philosophy to contemporary international relations.

Indeed, one of India's greatest strengths is its ability to constantly adapt, improvise and reinvent its traditions to accommodate modern developments and needs. This is seen above all in its rational secular ethos, something that is all the more remarkable when one takes into account the fact that this is a country where some 80 per cent of the population are devout Hindus, with its countless schools and branches, but which is also the national home of major Muslim, Sikh, Buddhist, Parsee, Jain, Christian and Jewish religious communities, along with the traditional and indigenous religious faiths still followed by some of the tribal peoples and others.

This diversity and tolerance helps to make India a great moral superpower. The country has huge military might and unlimited economic potential, yet the impact made by India and by people of Indian origin, from the South Pacific to North America, and from Britain to South Africa, results not from these factors, but from the richness of Indian culture, the strength of its example, the profundity of its philosophy, and the resilience of its people. There are, of course, examples where Indian culture and people of Indian origin have encountered resentment and hostility. Those displaying such a short-sighted attitude should think again. The Indian people do not come as conquerors. They come and they contribute - economically, politically, culturally and socially - and every time to the benefit and gain of the countries and peoples with whom they intersect.

India is a continuum. A country poised in every way to meet the challenges of the 21st century, with, for example, the world's largest pool of both computer programmers and graduate engineers, it firmly holds its place as an equal among the nations of the world, absorbing everything of value in the experiences of others, but never compromising for even a moment on all that is essentially Indian. This resolute but flexible defence of national values and traditions is an example to all the non-aligned nations and even to Europeans and North Americans as well.

This book strives to present a truthful picture of India. But we make no claim to detached objectivity. This is a sentimental journey, an evocation of India in all its richness, complexity and diversity.

We invite you to embark on this journey with us.

Arif Ali
July 1997

> *"Whenever there has been a conflict between my personal interests and the interests of the country as a whole, I have always placed the interests of the country above my personal claims. This is certain, that if the parties placed creed above country, our independence will be put in jeopardy a second time. This eventuality we must all resolutely guard against. We must be determined to defend our independence with the last drop of our blood."*

Dr. Babasaheb Ambedkar
Author of the Indian constitution

Introduction

INDIA IS a source of fascination, mystery and promise. Truly, it is a wealth of diversity. I became addicted to everything about India and her people right from the time of my first contact.

Therefore, when Arif Ali approached me to contribute an introduction to this latest title in Hansib's Nation series, I was delighted to do so.

Throughout my years of involvement with Indian people at home and abroad, I have been privileged to make innumerable friends and to benefit from their wisdom and philosophy of life which have taken shape and matured over five thousand years of unbroken civilisation.

The tremendous affection I feel for India and its people is something that I find difficult to convey adequately in words. It is, therefore, with special pleasure that I welcome a publication that articulates, in both text and photographs, the special feelings that I share with countless others.

This year, India celebrates its fiftieth anniversary of independence. This is but a moment in the life of such a timeless nation. Yet, in that precious moment, India has achieved so much in laying the foundations for its emergence as a global superpower in the 21st century - the ultimate "Asian Tiger", politically, economically, culturally, and morally.

Any worthwhile contribution to India's progress represents an important service to the whole of humanity. In this context I welcome *India - A Wealth of Diversity* for the contribution it will surely render.

Lady Maureen Thomas
July 1997

LEFT: **NEW DELHI**, *the capital of India*

7

Contents

OPPOSITE: **CARNIVAL REVELLER IN GOA**. *Carnival is celebrated by Christians, a third of the State's population.*

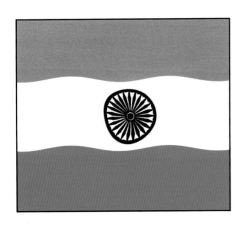

NATIONAL FLAG. *The Indian flag was designed as a symbol of freedom. The late Prime Minister Nehru called it a flag not only of freedom for the Indian people, but a symbol of freedom to all people. The flag is a horizontal tricolour in equal proportions of deep saffron on the top, white in the middle and dark green at the bottom. The ratio of the width to the length of the flag is two to three. In the centre of the white band, there is a wheel in navy blue to indicate the Dharma Chakra, the wheel of law in the Sarnath Lion Capital. Its diameter approximates the width of the white band and it has 24 spokes. The saffron stands for courage, sacrifice and the spirit of renunciation; the white for purity and truth; the green for faith and fertility.*

NATIONAL FLOWER - THE LOTUS. *The Lotus or waterlily is an aquatic plant of nymphaea with broad floating leaves and bright fragrant flowers that grow only in shallow water. The leaves and flowers float and have long stems that contain air spaces. The large attractive flowers have many petals overlapping in a symmetrical pattern. The root functions are carried out by rhizomes that fan out horizontally through the mud below the water. Lotuses, prized for their serene beauty, are delightful to behold as their blossoms open out on the surface of a pond. In India the sacred lotus is legendary and much folklore and religious mythology is woven around it.*

NATIONAL FRUIT - THE MANGO. *A fleshy fruit, eaten ripe or used green for pickles, of the tree mangifera indica, the mango is one of the most important and widely cultivated fruits of the tropical world. Its juicy fruit is a rich source of vitamins A, C and D. In India there are over 100 varieties of mangoes, in different sizes, shapes and colours. Mangoes have been cultivated in India from time immemorial. The poet Kalidasa sang their praises. Alexander the Great savoured their taste, as did the Chinese pilgrim Hieun Tsang. Akbar planted 100,000 mango trees in Darbhanga, known as Lakhi Bagh.*

NATIONAL BIRD - THE PEACOCK. *The species P. cristatus, is a native of India, and the male has striking plumage and upper tail converts marked with iridescent ocelli, able to expand its tail erect like a fan as ostentatious displays. Peacocks are related to pheasants. Found wild in India (and also domesticated in villages) they live in jungle lands near water. They were once bred for food but the hunting of peacocks is now banned in India. The peahen has no plumage. These birds do not sound as beautiful as they look - they have a harsh call.*

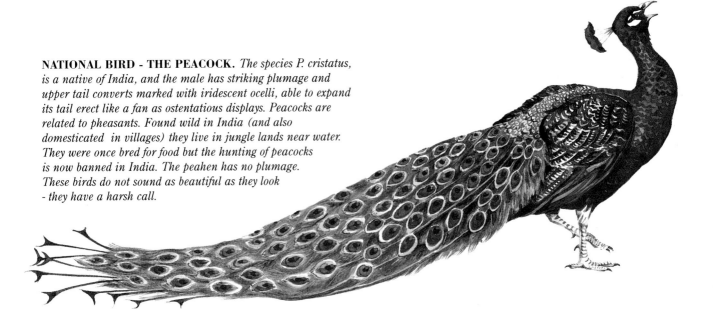

14

NATIONAL EMBLEM. *The National Emblem of India is a replica of the Lion of Sarnath, near Varanasi in Uttar Pradesh. The Lion Capital was erected in the third century BC by Emperor Ashoka to mark the spot where Buddha first proclaimed his gospel of peace and emancipation to the four corners of the universe. The National Emblem is therefore symbolic of contemporary India's reaffirmation of its ancient commitment to world peace and goodwill. The four lions (one hidden from view) - symbolising power, courage and confidence - rest on a circular abacus. The abacus is girded by four smaller animals - guardians of the four directions: the lion of the north, the elephant of the east, the horse of the south and the bull of the west. The abacus rests on a lotus in full bloom, exemplifying the fountainhead of life and creative inspiration. The motto 'Satyameva Jayate' inscribed below the emblem in Devanagari script means "truth alone triumphs".*

NATIONAL ANTHEM. *The words are taken from a Hindi poem by Rabindranath Tagore (pictured below):*

> *Jana-Gana-Mana-Adhinayaka, Jaya He*
> *Bharata Bhagya Vidhata*
> *Punjab-Sindhu-Gujarata-Maratha-*
> *Dravida-Utkala-Banga*
> *Vindhya-Himachala-Yamuna-Ganga*
> *Ucchhala-Jaladhi Taranga*
> *Tava Subha Name Jage*
> *Tava Subha Ashisha Mage*
> *Gahe Tava Yaya Gatha.*
> *Jana-Gana-Mangala Dayaka, Jaya He*
> *Bharata-Bhagya-Vidhata,*
> *Jaya He, Jaya He, Jaya He,*
> *Jaya Jaya Jaya, Jaya He*

The English translation of Tagore's rendering is:

> *Thou art the ruler of the minds of all people*
> *Dispenser of India's destiny.*
> *The name rouses the hearts of Punjab, Sind, Gujarat and Maratha*
> *Of the Dravid and Orissa and Bengali;*
> *It echoes in the hills of the Vindhyas and Himalayas,*
> *Mingles in the music of the Yamuna and Ganga*
> *And is chanted by the waves of the Indian Sea.*
> *They pray for thy blessings and sing thy praise*
> *The salvation of all people is in thy hand,*
> *Thou dispenser of India's destiny.*
> *Victory, victory, victory to thee.*

NATIONAL ANIMAL - THE TIGER

Large Asiatic carnivorous feline quadruped,
Panthera Tigris, maneless, of tawny yellow colour
with blackish transverse stripes and white belly,
proverbial for its power and magnificence.
There are very few tigers left in the world today. A
decade ago the tiger population in India had
dwindled to a few hundred. The Government of
India, under its Project Tiger programme, started
a massive effort to preserve the tiger population.
Today, thanks to this project, India's population
of tigers has considerably increased. The tiger
census is compiled by forest rangers using the
prints of the animal's distinctive pug mark to
avoid double counting and to ensure greater
accuracy. Outside the reserves, the tiger
population is still small. Poaching for tiger skin
and bones is a lucrative business that now poses
the greatest threat to the tigers' survival.

LEFT: **NATIONAL TREE - THE BANYAN**
Indian fig tree, Ficus bengalensis, whose branches root themselves like new trees over a large area. The roots then give rise to more trunks and branches. Because of this characteristic and its longevity, this tree is considered immortal and is an integral part of the myths and legends of India. Even today, the banyan tree is the focal point of rural life and the village council meets under its shade
The world's largest banyan, with a canopy covering 1.2 hectares, is in the Calcutta Botanical Gardens.

OPPOSITE: **A SADHU** *in the holy city of Pushkar, Rajasthan. A Sadhu is a celibate, who renounces the material world in pursuit of higher truths. Most travel the country and gather at the great pilgrimages and other important gatherings such as the Maya Kumbh Mela.*

ABOVE: *Shrines are lovingly dressed by the faithful*

RIGHT: **VARANASI**, *formerly Benares, on the Ganga is the most revered and most famous Hindu pilgrimage centre, and is regarded as the ideal place to breathe one's last. Varanasi - from the rivers Varuna and Asi - is also a centre of Sanskritic culture, more than 2,000 years old. There are more than a hundred ghats (riverside steps) at Varanasi, on the west bank of the Ganga. The ghats are for bathing and meditation. There are several burning ghats, principally Manikarnika and Harishchandra. Three Jain temples are situated in Bachraj Ghat. Two mosques - the Alamgir, built over a Vishnu temple, and the great mosque of Aurangzeb - are above the Panchganga Ghat. Here five rivers meet. Varanasi is close to Sarnath, where Buddha first preached his message of enlightenment twenty-five centuries ago.*

commanding the respect and esteem of his Hindu neighbours.

Akbar, the Mughal emperor, who wanted to become acquainted with the 'new' religion, invited some Jesuit Fathers to his court and gave them permission to baptise all who wished to become Christian. The very first church in the north, at Lahore, was built with his approval.

With the arrival of Protestant missions in the 18th century, Christianity began to permeate all strata of Indian life. The Christians helped in the propagation of modern western knowledge and education, and Indianised their lives by building churches in Indian architectural styles. They also set hymns to the tunes of Indian devotional music.

Almost 50 per cent of Christians are to be found in Tamil Nadu and Kerala. Christmas is a major holiday, and Christians play an important role in all spheres of Indian life.

ZOROASTRIANISM and JUDAISM

Another religious community which has enriched Indian life is the Zoroastrians, known as Parsis. When the Parsi followers of Zoroastrianism fled to India from religious persecution in Iran, they were given sanctuary in Gujarat by the Hindu king.

Followers of the great master, Zarathushtra, who was born in Medina in

BELOW: **HOLI** *is a popular and joyous Hindu festival, celebrated mainly in the north in February and March. Holi marks the end of winter. Participants try to cover each other with powder and coloured water. It is also considered spiritually beneficial to run across coals of fire.*

ABOVE: **RAMADAN** *is the major Muslim festival, marking the end of a 30-day, dawn-to-dusk fast. Mosques are brightly lit and decorated for the occasion.*

about 600 BC, their holy book is the *Zend Avesta*, a collection of the sayings of the Zarathushtra. Generous lovers of nature and flowers, particularly the rose, the Parsis brought with them their agricultural and horticultural skills and later on played a remarkable role in the political, industrial and economic development of India, particularly over the last two centuries.

Their holy book contains some of the most noble philosophic and metaphysical principles and an elevating ethical code. They subscribe to a simple yet complex belief: live and let live and view human relationships dispassionately.

Judaism is one of the world's oldest organised religions, its origin being attributed to Abraham about 4,000 years ago. Their arrival in India predates the beginning of the Christian era. The oldest communities are the Bene-Israel, of the coastal areas of Maharastra, and the Jews of Cochin. They were persecuted wherever they went with practically the sole exception of India and they remember this with gratitude.

The Vedic dictum: "Truth is one, the wise call it by many names" has largely dictated India's unique co-existence of many faiths.

Festivals

INDIAN HOLIDAYS AND FESTIVALS are determined by the Indian lunar calendar and, to a significant extent, by the different religious influences. Along with national public holidays, there are many other regional or local events observed as holidays in any of the 25 States.

JANUARY - FEBRUARY

Republic Day (January 26th)

All State capitals celebrate the anniversary of the Republic of India (1950), particularly in Delhi where there is a mighty military parade.

Pongal

A four-day Tamil festival marks the end of the harvest season. It is observed on the first day of the Tamil month of Thai (middle of January). In Andhra Pradesh the festival is known as Makar Sankranti.

Vasant Panchami

A Spring Festival, held in January where people wear yellow clothes. In West Bengal, Saraswati, the goddess of learning, is honoured.

FEBRUARY - MARCH

Holi

Hindu festival, to mark the end of winter. Coloured water and powder are thrown. This festival is known as Rangapanchami in Maharashtra.

Shivaratri

A day of fasting is dedicated to Lord Shiva, who danced the tandava on this day.

MARCH - APRIL

Mahavir Jayanti

Jain festival marking the birth of Mahavira, the founder of Jainism.

Ramanavami

The birth of Rama, an incarnation of Vishnu.

Good Friday

The Christian festival celebrating the resurrection of Christ.

Gangaur

A Rajasthani festival honouring Siva and Parvati.

APRIL - MAY

Baisakhi

A Sikh festival to commemorate the day on which Guru Gobind Singh founded the Khalsa.

MAY - JUNE

Buddha Jayanti

The Buddha's birth, enlightenment and attainment of nirvana.

JUNE - JULY

Rath Yatra (Car festival)

Lord Jagannath's (Krishna) great temple chariot makes its stately journey from his temple in Puri, Orissa.

JULY - AUGUST

Naag Panchami

A festival dedicated to Ananta, the serpent upon whose coils Vishnu rested between universes. Snakes are supposed to have power over the monsoon rainfall and keep evil from homes.

Raksha Brandhan (Narial Purnima)

A celebration on the full-moon day of the Hindu month of Sravana (July/August), when girls fix amulets known as rakhis to their brothers' wrists to protect them in the coming year. The brothers reciprocate with gifts.

Drupka Teshi

A Buddhist festival celebrating the first teaching given by the Buddha.

AUGUST - SEPTEMBER

Independence Day (August 15th)

Celebrates the anniversary of India's independence.

Ganesh Chaturthi

A festival held on the fourth day of the Hindu month Bhadra (August/September) dedicated to Ganesh. As Ganesh is the god of wisdom and prosperity, Ganesh Chaturthi is considered to be the most auspicious day of the year. It is considered unlucky to look at the moon on this day.

Janmashtami

The anniversary of Krishna's birth is a national holiday with Agra, Bombay and Mathura (his birthplace) the main centres of celebration.

Shravan Purnima

After a day-long fast, high-caste Hindus replace the sacred thread which they always wear looped over their left shoulder.

SEPTEMBER - OCTOBER

Dussehra

A ten-day festival to celebrate Durga's victory over the buffalo-headed demon Mahishasura.

Gandhi Jayanti (October 2nd)

The most popular festival. A solemn celebration of Mahatma Gandhi's birthday.

OCTOBER - NOVEMBER

Diwali (or Deepavali)

The happiest Hindu festival, celebrated on the 15th day of Kartika. Diwali has also become the Festival of Sweets and is also celebrated by the Jains as their New Year's Day.

Govardhana Puja

Hindu festival dedicated to the cow.

NOVEMBER - DECEMBER

Nanak Jayanti

The birthday of Guru Nanak, the founder of Sikh religion.

Christmas Day (December 25th)

Christian Festival marking the birth of Christ.

The dates of the Muslim holidays are not fixed. The main Muslim festivals are:

Ramadan

The most important Muslim festival in this 30-day dawn-to-dusk fast commemorating the prophet Mohammed when he received his revelation from Allah.

Id-ul-Fitr

This festival celebrates the end of Ramadan, the Muslim month of fasting.

Id-ul-Zuhura

This festival commemorates Abraham's attempt to sacrifice his son.

Muharram

A ten-day festival commemorating the martyrdom of Mohammed's grandson, Imam Hussain.

Milad-un-Nabi

A festival celebrating the birth of Mohammed.

OPPOSITE, ABOVE AND NEXT PAGE: **GOMATESHVARA** - *or Bahubali - is an 18-metre high monolithic statue on Indragiri, a granite hill. The statue is associated with the Mauryan emperor Chandragupta, who in accordance with a Jain custom, had fasted to death on the hill, which was first named Chandragiri to record the arrival of Jainism in south India The hill has more than 500 steps. Bahubali the son of Adinath nearly kills his brother in a fierce fight over their inheritance. Bahubali regrets his action and, full of remorse, turns his back on the vices of greed, jealousy and violence. Thus, he attains moksha, or rebirth. Meditating in solitude he also advances to the state of kevalajnana, a high peak of knowledge. The statue was built in the tenth century by King Chavundaraya and overlooks the town of Sravanabelagola in Karnataka. One of the world's tallest monolithic statues, it attracts pilgrims and visitors from all over the world, especially during the Gomatshevra festival.* **MAHAMASTAKBHISHEKA,** *the ritual annointment ceremony, is held over several days once every twelve years, the date determined by precise astrological calculations. The ceremony is conducted in complete silence. On the final day, from a specially erected scaffold, Bahubali is showered with thousands of pots of milk and ghee, coloured water, cane juice, saffron, sugar, almonds, poppy seeds, gold, silver and flowers.*

The Long March to Freedom

S HORTLY before midnight on August 14, 1947, Jawaharlal Nehru, one of the heroic leaders of the Freedom Struggle, propelled and motivated by two simple but deeply emotive, peremptory and uncompromising words, *QUIT INDIA*, addressed his country's Legislative Assembly. The non-violent actions to force the occupying power to leave Indian territory, shook the mighty British Empire as it had never been shaken before, setting in train the process of decolonisation in the rest of Asia, Africa and the Caribbean.

In a poignant speech, suffused with poetry, emotion and magnanimity, Nehru, one of the world's great orators, statesmen and historians, brought tears to the eyes of hundreds of millions of his fellow countrymen, when he said: "Long years ago we made a tryst with destiny, and now the time comes when we shall redeem the pledge, not wholly or in full measure but very substantially. At the stroke of the midnight hour, while the world sleeps, India will wake to life and freedom."

Thus was born independent India under the Prime Ministership of Jawaharlal Nehru.

It was a wonderful moment, somewhat marred by the bloodshed and upheaval surrounding the partition of the sub-continent, from which emerged Pakistan, under the leadership of Mohammed Ali Jinnah.

The next day, Lord Mountbatten was sworn in as the Governor-General of the 'Dominion' of India, a status which Nehru and many others felt was incompatible with a free, sovereign and independent nation.

The colourful Durbar Hall, the setting of many splendid British ceremonies, now saw what some commentators described as an *"Indian occasion for the Indian people"*. The Indians claimed their birthright when the British flag gave way to the Indian national flag, which appropriately for a secular nation, was designed by a Muslim, Badr-ud-Din Tyabji. With a touch worthy of this defining moment in history, Jawaharlal Nehru's car was adorned by a smaller version of the Indian national flag especially made for the Prime Minister by Tyabji's wife.

The *Quit India* movement was the most decisive phase of the struggle for independence, prominently highlighted in the international and national media of the day. However, uprisings, upheavals and non-violent and violent conflicts, roundtable conferences and dialogues between representatives of the Raj and the leaders of the freedom movement, from the moment the British penetrated the sub-continent in the 18th century until the dying moments of foreign rule, were all part of a long drawn-out and continuous resistance.

The *Quit India* movement, masterminded by Mohandas Karamchand Gandhi, was based on non-violence, but other struggles for the liberation of the country were based on what their leaders, especially Subhas Chandra Bose, implied was constructive violence.

While some of the traditional rulers were too weak to oppose the British invasion, others, especially the best known of them, Haidar Ali and his son, Tipu Sultan, won many important battles against the British, with Tipu forcing treaties on the enemy. Then there was the legendary Rani of Jhansi, a woman who fought like a lioness to restore India to Indian rule.

The so-called 'Indian Mutinty' of 1857, which many Indian and international historians regard as the First Indian War of Independence, came close to bringing down the curtains on the British Empire in India. Even some British military experts have said that if the war had not been confined to the west of India, and the rest of the country had risen against alien rule, the British would have been forced to flee.

The last and final phase of the Indian struggle for independence, however, cannot be isolated from the condition of India before the coming of British imperialism. The previous Empire builders, who were to make an even greater impact on India than the British, were the Muslims. The Arabs at the height of their power - they had conquered Spain, itself by no means an imperialist lightweight, and had brought the area right to the borders of Mongolia under their control, bringing with them the gains of a new, brilliant and remarkable civilisation - only conquered a part of India, Sind in the north west in 712 AD. They never went further.

The Arabs were not to return. India was invaded by other Muslims from the north west, but they were absorbed, and soon became as Indian as the Ganga. It was left to another great Muslim civilisation, ironically descended from the mightiest non-Muslim empire of the 12th century AD, and led by the greatest military leader of all time, the ruthless Genghis Khan, to significantly alter the Indian political, cultural, social and religious landscape.

A descendant of Genghis, Babur, a Turco-Mongol prince from the famous and fearsome Timurid line in central Asia, and believed to be the great Khan's grandson, was the first of the Grand Mughals. He was the founder of the Mughal Empire of India whose rule was mainly confined to north India. The south, the home of great cities like the beautiful and imposing Vijayanagar, and great civilisations like the Chola and the Pandyan, remained largely independent and sovereign.

The Mughal Empire, highly accomplished in the arts, in literature, music, administration, cuisines and military prowess, ruled for over 200 fruitful years. There were other Muslim players on the Indian scene, like the Turks and Afghans. They also became an integral part of India, intermarrying and mixing with the people, and willingly being absorbed into the greater national family. The Mughals also succumbed to the inevitable process of absorption, making an indispensable contribution to the evolution of the secular Indian way of life. Many of the Afghans, Turks and Mughal rulers and their sons married Hindu women. It would not be correct, therefore, to speak of a Muslim invasion of India. Islam, incidentally, had come to India long before the political conquests by Arabs, Afghans, Turks and Mughals.

But, however inviting an India, at a low ebb, was to the Europeans, it was remote and inaccessible because they were not yet masters of the sea. But at a crucial juncture, the decline of the south Indian naval power of the mighty Chola Kingdom, opened up brighter prospects for the predatory European powers. Spain, Portugal and Britain were devoting huge resources to the development of their navies, with Britannia eventually ruling the waves and equipping herself for the great adventure in her then incipient imperial history, the conquest of India.

The year 1615 was a major turning point in the misfortunes of the sub-continent. That year, the British defeated the Portuguese in a naval encounter in Indian territorial waters. The Mughals, under Jehangir, were not prepared for the events that followed.

Sir Thomas Roe presented himself at Jehangir's court in 1615 as the Ambassador of James I of England. Diplomatic protocol was not as refined as it is today, and the ambassador obtained permission to start a factory in Surat. A British presence was also established in Madras (now Chennai) in 1639. Strangely, the British had operated largely in the commercial sector for over a hundred years, and not much notice had been taken of them.

However, observing the growing weakness of Aurungzeb, the British tried to increase their influence and entrench themselves by waging war. Aurungzeb had little difficulty in crushing them.

However, Aurungzeb was a short-sighted ruler whose imposition of harsh taxes on the people led to many revolts, first on a local scale and then nationally. It was the Marathas, under the wise statesman and shrewd military leader, Shivaji, who destroyed Mughal power. Shivaji also attacked the English factories in Surat as part of a larger strategy to rid India of their presence.

The well-organised Marathas built on the legacy left by the revered Shivaji who had died in 1680, and became the dominant power in India.

In the late 18th century there were four contenders for power - two Indian and two foreign. The patriots were the Marathas and Haidar Ali and his son, Tipu Sultan, in the south. The foreigners were the French and the British. It seemed at this stage that there was no power strong enough to stand in the way of an eventual Maratha victory.

Unfortunately for the Marathas, they suffered a serious setback as they spread themselves over north India. In 1761, an Afghan leader defeated some of their best regiments and gravely weakened Maratha power at a time when they needed to be at their best to realise their dream of a free and united India.

This setback for the Marathas was good news for the East India Company, which having established itself under the patronage of the Mughals to which it paid tribute, now felt it could expand without any serious resistance. The Company had started as a trading post, but gradually entrenched itself as a political and territorial power.

In 1757, Clive, a British official, won the Battle of Plassey with the help of treacherous elements. Many regard 1757 as the year in which the British Empire effectively penetrated India after taking Bengal and Bihar without much of a fight.

In the south, the French and the British fought for territory. The French lost. In the late 18th century the fate of India rested in the hands of the Maratha confederacy, Haider Ali in the South, and the British.

Despite Clive's victory, the Marathas were by far the superior power, their writ running over western and central India right up to Delhi. And they were still a very formidable fighting machine. Then the British also had to cope with Haider Ali and Tipu Sultan. Father and son had defeated the British in several encounters and had very nearly succeeded in destroying the East India Company. Haider Ali was a visionary leader, who knew only too well that British power could only be destroyed by a strong Indian navy and a united front of all the regional forces, with the Marathas an indispensable, key element.

Haider Ali had started to build his own navy after capturing the Maldives, and appealed to other Indian rulers for unity but he was forced to fight alone. His son, too, did not secure the co-operation of other Indian rulers.

The British eventually won control of India with the help of luck and fluke. They had been defeated many times by Haider Ali and Tipu, the Marathas, Sikhs and Gurkhas but they still managed to hang on.

However, it was not all down to good luck and fluke. In the end their unity against a divided India, and their superior naval power told heavily in their favour.

What was India like before the path-breaking English industrial revolution? India was an advanced manufacturing nation which exported its products to the world. She had a sophisticated banking system which networked efficiently with similar systems in the rest of Asia. Emerging merchant capital could possibly have led to the transformation of the leading industrial business houses in the country into multinationals. In the light of the modern emphasis on information technology, it is significant that in the 18th century large numbers of manufacturing and trading centres had a swift and efficient system of communicating business and sensitive political information.

India also had a lively and thriving ship-building industry and during the Napoleonic wars its shipyards had produced one of the British Royal Navy's flagships. There is little doubt that, industrially, commercially and financially, India had reached a very developed stage before the Industrial Revolution.

The first serious and most threatening challenge to British domination in India was the May, 1857 revolt at Meerut, the First Indian War of Independence. It was not confined to soldiers and spread rapidly to become a popular uprising in Delhi, the United Provinces (UP) and parts of central India and Bihar. Both Hindus and Muslims fought side by side in this great revolt against the common enemy. There were some brilliant leaders in this guerrilla war. Feroz Shah was one them. Tantia Topi was another. He led many surprise charges against British troops and moved out of danger with equal speed and skill. However, the odds were against him and he fell in battle. The most loved of the leaders was Lakshmi Bai, Rani of Jhansi, a beautiful girl of 20 who died sword in hand. The English general who fought against her described Lakshmi Bai, as "the best and bravest of the rebel leaders." The Indians were shocked by the cruelty of the repression. The British *Times* newspaper called for the "extermination of every Hindoo and Mussalman" in India.

After this first war of independence, the British moved quickly to consolidate their rule. They devised and executed a master plan to prevent other uprisings and wars: they divided India into two. What was called British India was under the rule of the Delhi Viceroy, while the 550 princely states, nominally ruled by their princes, were effectively British satrapies.

In the closing stages of the 18th century, many Indians sought to express their grievances against British rule through constitutional means, primarily the press. The British, however, regarded a free press as

Mohandas Karamchand Gandhi:

A Prince among men

Over a billion words have been written about Gandhi, one of the principal architects of the non-violent Quit India movement, barrister-at-law, social and educational reformer, dietitian, educationalist, pioneering champion of alternative medicine and ardent advocate of morality in political, business and religious life.

Most of the writing is hagiographic, while some of it, particularly in the land of his birth, is quite critical. As for Gandhi himself, although assertive, he was never an egotist, and always insisted that he was no saint but a mere mortal.

Indeed, Gandhi relished debate and gave as good as he got. He argued with Tagore about industrialisation, the latter being all for modernisation, while Gandhi lauded the merits of what he called the cottage industry, anticipating the slogan, 'small is beautiful' by 75 years. He waged a fierce polemic with Saklatvala, the British communist MP of Indian origin, and he charmingly teased Nehru about his passionate socialism, making it clear that he did not believe in regimentation but was in favour of the free market. However, Gandhi insisted that those who made money from the toil and labour of others, should consider their wealth not as their own, but to be held in trust, with the profits used for the benefit of the underprivileged. This would imply that Gandhi, like Adam Smith, the father of market economics, did not believe in *laissez faire* extremes, and favoured state intervention to help ensure social and economic justice.

In South Africa where he practiced as a young lawyer, Gandhi, concerned by some of the sharp practices of the Indian merchant class, told their leaders that they should behave ethically. This man who regarded money with disdain, an inconvenient and unclean necessity in a cash-nexus society, and spent his own income on social work, publishing and other good

"Generations to come will scarce believe that a one such as this, ever in flesh and blood, walked upon this earth."

Albert Einstein
January, 1948

"I shall work for an India in which the poorest shall feel that it is their country, in whose making they have an effective voice, an India in which there shall be no high class and low class of people, an India in which all communities shall live in perfect harmony.... There can be no room in such an India for the curse of untouchability or the curse of intoxicating drinks and drugs....Women will enjoy the same rights as men....This is the India of my dream."

Mohandas K. Gandhi

causes, was deeply shocked when the merchants replied that they would never be successful if they believed in ethics and fairplay!

Gandhi had more success, however, in persuading would be litigants to settle their disputes by arbitration rather than recourse to law, because the only people to benefit from conflicts in the court would be lawyers. He is probably one of the few lawyers of distinction to have so bravely exposed the exploitative nature of 'legal practice'. Gandhi also drew attention to the ill feeling that such cases often produced.

In one such widely publicised dispute in South Africa between two branches of the same family, Gandhi successfully persuaded them not to go to law, but to accept the decision of an arbiter. Both parties expressed their gratitude to Gandhi, not only for saving them unnecessary expense, but also avoiding a painful, acrimonious and bitter separation.

Gandhi, who was fanatical about cleanliness, never spared the Indians of South Africa, particularly the merchant classes, for their generally poor standards of hygiene. He set a personal example by cleaning the toilets of his home, office and printing plant.

In one of his first public pronouncements on his return to India, Gandhi launched an uncharacteristically vitriolic attack on Indians for their lack of public hygiene, and told them in no uncertain terms to revise their cynical attitude that cleaning latrines was strictly an occupation for the so-called 'untouchables'. Nothing, not even the insolence of British officials, angered this gentle advocate of non-violent resistance more than the filth and dirt of Indian streets and markets. On one occasion, a clearly angry and impatient Gandhi grabbed a broom and proceeded, much to the shame and embarrassment of the so-called upper castes, to clean a Mumbai public lavatory.

A strict vegetarian, Mohandas was not particularly enamoured of Indian food and seems to have had a dread of the nation's spices. Indeed, he gave up curries for a Western, particularly German Lutheran inspired diet of nuts, fresh fruit, milk, freshly-made pure orange juice, groundnuts and salads of ripe and unripe bananas, lemons, tomatoes, grapes and olive oil. He believed that one should eat for reasons of health and energy rather than out of sensuousness or gluttony.

Gandhi's *Satyaghra* philosophy was an eclectic mix. The men who had the profoundest impact on that philosophy were Rajchandra, an obscure but brilliant Indian with "an inexhaustible knowledge of the Hindu scriptures"; the Russian, Leo Tolstoy, author of 'The Kingdom of God Is Within You'; and the eminent English art critic, John Ruskin, author of 'Unto This Last'. Gandhi generously acknowledged his huge debt to these two great works and the writings of the Americans, Henry D. Thoreau and Ralph Waldo Emerson, in the shaping of his own spiritual outlook, so succinctly articulated in one of his earliest essays, 'Civil Disobedience'.

Gandhi was as Indian as the Himalayas, but he was also a man whose thoughts, beliefs and actions transcended national and international barriers. He read widely and voraciously, not just works by Indian writers, but also by some equally great Asian and Western writers. He was a Hindu, but never a narrow or dogmatic one, embracing all the faiths including Islam, Christianity, Buddhism, Jainism, Zoroastrianism and Judaism. This was movingly evident in many of the hymns that were sung at his regular prayer sessions.

He particularly admired the literary skill and wisdom of Tolstoy who had also renounced worldly pleasures in pursuit of the higher truths. Long

Gandhi as a young man

before Gandhi became famous, the very perceptive Tolstoy, one of the finest judges of human character, predicted that the "Hindu from Natal" was destined for greatness. In South Africa, Gandhi founded the Tolstoy Farm in honour of his spiritual and literary hero. Tolstoy, however, was painfully frank in their correspondence, conducted between Gandhi and the Russian when Mohandas was still in South Africa.

Tolstoy told Gandhi that it was preposterous that the British, who had originally established a commercial company, could enslave a nation of 200 million. He added: "Tell this to a man free from superstition and he will fail to grasp what these words mean. What does it mean that 30,000 people, not athletes, but rather weak and ill-looking, have enslaved 200 millions of vigorous, strong, clever, freedom-loving people? Do not the figures alone make it clear that not the English, but the Hindus themselves are the cause of their slavery?"

Gandhi was to follow much of Tolstoy's advice of non-co-operation with the "violent deeds of the British administration, of the law courts, of the collection of taxes and what is most important, of the soldiers." He said with such non-cooperation "no one in the world can enslave you."

Gandhi first experimented with non-violent resistance in South Africa with some effectiveness because of the discipline, dedication and hatred of oppression of the indentured labourers. It was a struggle from which the Indian merchant class stood aloof, indeed trying hard to ingratiate themselves with the white, racist government by asking to be classified as "white" despite the fact that only a few of them were "fair" and the rest "Khaki brown". The merchants had always described themselves as Arabs, probably because light-skinned Syrian and Lebanese immigrants were treated as white people. Gandhi, however, advised them not to make fools of themselves by weakening the struggle against a cruelly oppressive regime, which if anything, hated the merchant class even more than it did the poor and wretched indentured labourers.

In the successful struggle against attempts to impose the Pass Laws on the Indians of South Africa, Gandhi often clashed with the pro-imperialist Boer Leader, General J.C. Smuts. Despite the betrayal and the deceit of the government in which Smuts was a minister, the two men got on reasonably well, with Smuts even telling Gandhi that the Indians were, a hardworking and highly intelligent race with a remarkable civilisation, superior to whites.

When Smuts learned of the assassination of Mohandas Karamchand Gandhi, he paid this memorably eloquent tribute to his former adversary: "A prince among men has passed away."

The Nehrus:

Not a conventional dynasty but a family of democratically elected leaders

IT IS unfortunate that the superficial Western media has propagated, to an excessive degree, the concept of the 'Nehru Dynasty'.

A dynasty, such as the Qing dynasty in China, for instance, or the Windsors in Britain, is not elected. They are there because of the mystical concept of "divine right." In contrast, India, where free and fair elections are held regularly, the people decide who will rule them. It is interesting to recall that Indira Gandhi, an important member of the so-called 'Nehru Dynasty', was rejected by the electorate in the 70s and voted back into power in the subsequent election.

Most of the Nehrus, it would appear, were not only aristocrats by birth - cultivated Kashmiri Brahmins - but they, especially Motilal, Jawaharlal's father, Jawaharlal himself, and his daughter, Indira, also belonged to the aristocracy of the intelligentsia. Rajiv Gandhi may not have been considered to be in the same intellectual league as his mother and grandfather, but for a young, unambitious but contented airline pilot, without any apparent interest in politics, suddenly thrust into the leadership cockpit, he proved surprisingly mature and skilled in domestic and international politics.

Sanjay, in whom his doting mother, Indira, had placed all her hopes, would have been the last person to claim that he was an intellectual. On the contrary. He seems to have consciously rebelled against his revered grandfather's dreamy scholarship, poetic reveries and Hamlet-like weighing of the pros and cons of an argument, and confidently proclaimed himself a practical man, a man of action. But he also shared with his grandfather an adventurous spirit, and though Jawaharlal would have mourned Sanjay's youthful end, he would have been proud of the manner of his passing - defying the gods, the machine and fate as he engaged in the flying stunts that killed him.

Motilal Nehru, Rajiv and Sanjay's great grandfather, was the man who launched the historical phenomenon that so powerfully changed the fortunes and destiny of India. But he never did so consciously, indeed this hedonistic but very able lawyer with a large house, a comfortable income and strong bourgeois inclinations, was largely indifferent to nationalist politics. In his palatial home, Anand Bhavan, in Allahabad, which he had bought in 1900, Motilal entertained lavishly, enjoyed scotch whisky, was westernised and had many of the luxuries that seemed to be the effortless birthright of the privileged of that age, not just in India but in Europe and North America. Cars were just coming into fashion and Motilal owned an impressive model, chauffeur-driven of course. His impeccable sartorial tastes were much admired, and he even sent his separate white collars, very fashionable among the British and Indian upper class of that time, to select establishments in London to be cleaned and starched.

The boy Jawaharlal was the apple of his father's eye. Motilal sent him to Harrow and Cambridge, where the young man performed with the excellence expected of him. Nehru also enrolled at the Inner Temple, from which he was called to the Bar. The father's fond hope was that his son would follow him into law and inherit one of the best practices in the country. But the sensitive, idealistic and politically conscious Jawaharlal was more interested in the liberation of his country than in amassing wealth.

Motilal was upset not because he disapproved of nationalist politics, but because he could not bear the thought of his only son, who had been brought up in the most extravagant luxury, being subjected to the harsh rigours of the prison cells that the British had built to deal with troublesome nationalists. Motilal even slept on a mat on the bare, concrete floors of an unused room in his mansion in a melodramatic but touching attempt to gauge the level of discomfort his son would have to endure. He also tried to get Mahatma Gandhi to dissuade Jawaharlal from his chosen path. But when the son showed no sign of back-tracking, the father rejected his Saville Row suits, donned national dress and joined the Resistance. It was an amazing transformation.

THE HOUSE OF NEHRU: *Jawaharal Nehru, Indira Gandhi and Rajiv Gandhi*

Jawaharlal married Kamala (nee Kaul) in 1916. She was a frail beauty and gave birth to a daughter, Indira, in 1917. Kamala saw little of her husband, Jawaharlal, after the birth of their daughter as Nehru travelled the country to rally the villagers to the Great Cause and was frequently jailed for his many acts of defiance. Nehru was shattered when his wife died in 1936 in a Swiss clinic. Indira was now the centre of his life. He had started writing his famous letters to the girl, when she was five-years-old, on a number of topics, some facetious and light-hearted, others full of practical advice and many on the progress of the Resistance. These letters, written between 1922 and 1939, mostly during his prison years, are a *tour de force* of interpretation and analysis of the history of India, that of Europe, the emergence of European fascism and Nazism, and equally brilliant, learned and informative appraisals of modern and old works of English and European literature.

Indira went to a finishing school in Switzerland, studied at a British college for girls and went on to Cambridge, but there is no doubt that the major educational, social, political and cultural influence in her life was her extremely well-read and clever father, who devoured books in the solitude of his prison with amazing speed, and wrote about world events with the facility and expertise of a master scholar, historian and critic.

Like her father, Indira, who was Prime Minister of her country for 16 years, was a socialist who cared deeply about the poor of India and sought throughout her political career to improve their lives.

She also staunchly upheld the non-aligned principles of her father, an anti-racist and anti-

imperialist to his last. She maintained, like her father before her, and like her son Rajiv, after her, the fiercely proud and dignified independent foreign policy that won India, an important regional power, the respect of the world. India, from the moment of her emergence as a free and sovereign nation, had resolved that she would never be a camp follower, never be bullied by powerful ideologues of left or right, and would never remain neutral in the face of evil or be passive whenever and wherever regional or international peace was threatened.

India's non-aligned, anti-racist, anti-imperialist, anti-colonial, policies, some times bitterly resented by the big powers, especially when they were exposed of hypocrisy and double standards, has been, as history has shown, an indispensable bulwark against tyranny and war. India's insistence on the importance of peaceful resolutions of conflict, prevented several wars, possibly nuclear ones, while bringing others to a timely close.

Despite British and US arrogance in the Korean War, the then Labour Foreign Secretary, Ernest Bevin, appealed to India, which had cordial and influential relations with China, to broker a peace.

India also helped bring a speedy end to the illegal British-French and Israeli Occupation of the Suez Canal. Again the British, who had been so critical of India's non-aligned stance, found themselves relying on the good offices of the Indians to rescue them from their folly.

A year before his assassination, Rajiv Gandhi, launched the fearsome Indian rocket, Agni, purely for defensive purposes. This gave India entree to the select rocket club of the Soviet Union, Britain,

France, China and the United States. Rajiv disclosed at the launch that he had received a letter from George Bush, the President of the US, warning him against going ahead. Rajiv made it emphatically clear that India was master of its own affairs and did not take orders from any other nation, however powerful that nation may be. And Rajiv added with that much photographed endearing schoolboy grin: "I told Bush to go to hell."

Rajiv was his mother's son, his grandfather's grandson and an Indian patriot to the bone. In their time, both Jawaharlal and Indira had to deal with some self-opinionated world leaders in this firm and unbending manner. When Richard Nixon and Harold Wilson tried to warn Indira Gandhi against taking action to prevent the uncontrollable flood of refugees into India during the upheavals in the then East Pakistan, that led to the creation of Bangladesh, Mrs Gandhi defiantly took the requisite action. With the burden to house, clothe and feed them falling on the Indians, Mrs Gandhi gave her army instructions to stop the rot.

Similarly at the Bahamas Commonwealth Summit in the 1980s when British Prime Minister Margaret Thatcher was advocating a 'constructive dialogue' with the apartheid regime, Rajiv is said to have told her straight to her face: "We are not interested in what you think, we will go ahead and deal with the problem ourselves." The Australians and Canadians lined up firmly behind Rajiv.

Also at that conference, Zimbabwean leader Robert Mugabe complained to Rajiv about the murderous raids regularly being made into his country by the apartheid army. They killed with impunity and destroyed valuable property, seriously undermining the delicate agricultural and industrial infrastructure. This complaint was made to Rajiv not at an official session but in an aside during an adjournment. Listening in was Thatcher and other members of the British delegation. Rajiv reportedly told Mugabe: "Look, all you have to do when this happens again is give me a call and I'll send the Indian Air force backed by some ground troops. They won't stop at the South African border but go right into Pretoria to finish the job." Whether or not Mrs Thatcher phoned Pretoria, warning them not to play with fire, it seems that the message got home as there were no more raids into Zimbabwe.

Indeed, long before the world imposed economic, cultural and sports sanctions on South Africa, Nehru, in 1948, withdrew the Indian High Commissioner from South Africa, and unilaterally broke off all diplomatic relations, imposing a total boycott of the racist state. He told members of the Indian community in South Africa: "You are not Indians but Africans and must identify with the oppressed people. If you do not do so you must suffer the consequences, India has no responsibility for you." The vast majority of Indians took Nehru's message to heart.

Mrs Gandhi and Rajiv, too, with similarly strong anti-racist outlooks, were also held in the highest esteem and respect by the African people and their leaders.

With so many fissiparous and fragmentary tendencies in that country, pulling this way and that and often threatening the unity of the great secular, democratic state of India, the Nehrus were the bulwark against communal and provincial bigotry. They went out of their way to address the legitimate political and linguistic grievances of people in India's southern states, and led by example, particularly in their warm recognition of the south's many academic, technical, scientific, professional and diplomatic talents.

Sadly, too many of Nehru's people still think of themselves as Gujaratis, Bengalis etc first and Indians second. In contrast, Jawaharlal, Indira and Rajiv were first and foremost Indians and they practised what they preached. When Mrs Gandhi was told by her security advisers to replace the Sikh guard who was later to assassinate her, she refused on the ground that that would not be merely a sign of fear, but, more seriously, an encouragement of communal bigotry.

Nehru was an agnostic, a man of reason, who saw the Indian future in terms of science, technology and engineering. He believed that only by harnessing these assets to the concept of Five Year Plans would India make headway in terms of overcoming the nation's poverty and backwardness, perpetuated by colonial domination. He never suffered fools gladly, and hated inefficiency and unpunctuality. On a wall behind his desk were the words that sent a frisson of fear down the spines of many a Minister and bureaucrat: "I am not interested in excuses. I am interested in the thing done."

Nehru unleashed his fierce temper on the charlatans who exploited rituals and superstition for their own gain. He was equally unforgiving to those who engaged in excessive deference to the mighty of the earth. On one occasion, when a man fell at his feet, Nehru's angry retort summed up his antipathy to such outmoded conventions: "Get up you fool, if you don't I'll kick you."

Harsh words, but as they say one sometimes has to be cruel to be kind, especially when you are an egalitarian with a passionate belief in equality and progress, as all the members of this truly outstanding, talented, patriotic and democratic family have been.

What was this India that possessed me...?

DURING these years of thought and activity my mind has been full of India, trying to understand her and to analyse my own reactions towards her. I went back to my childhood days and tried to remember what I felt like then, what vague shape this conception took in my growing mind, and how it was moulded by fresh experience. Sometimes it receded into the background, but it was always there, slowly changing, a queer mixture derived from old story and legend and modern fact. It produced a sensation of pride in me as well as that of shame, for I was ashamed of much that I saw around me, of superstitious practices, of outworn ideas, and, above all, our subject and poverty-stricken state.

As I grew up and became engaged in activities which promised to lead to India's freedom, I became obsessed with the thought of India. What was this India that possessed me and beckoned to me continually, urging me to action so that we might realise some vague but deeply-felt desire of our hearts? The initial urge came to me, I suppose, through pride, both individual and national, and the desire, common to all men, to resist another's domination and have freedom to live the life of our choice. It seemed monstrous to me that a great country like India, with a rich and immemorial past, should be bound hand and foot to a far-away island which imposed its will upon her. It was still more monstrous that this forcible union had resulted in poverty and degradation beyond measure. That was reason enough for me and for others to act.

But it was not enough to satisfy the questioning that arose within me. What is this India, apart from her physical and geographical aspects? What did she represent in the past? What gave strength to her then? How did she lose that old strength? And has she lost it completely? Does she represent anything vital now, apart from being the home of a vast number of human beings? How does she fit into the modern world?

This wider international aspect of the problem grew upon me as I realised more and more how isolation was both undesirable and impossible. The future that took shape in my mind was one of intimate co-operation, politically, economically, and culturally, between India and the other countries of the world. But before the future came there was the present, and behind the present lay the long and tangled past, out of which the present had grown. So to the past I looked for understanding.

India was in my blood and there was much in her that instinctively thrilled me. And yet I approached her almost as an alien critic, full of

JAWAHARLAL NEHRU
The Discovery of India

dislike for the present as well as for many of the relics of the past that I saw. To some extent I came to her via the West, and looked at her as a friendly Westerner might have done. I was eager and anxious to change her outlook and appearance and give her the garb of modernity. And yet doubts arose within me. Did I know India? - I who presumed to scrap much of her past heritage? There was a great deal that had to be scrapped, that must be scrapped; but surely India could not have been what she undoubtedly was, and could not have continued a cultured existence for thousands of years, if she had not possessed something very vital and enduring, something that was worthwhile. What was this something?

I stood on a mound of Mohenjo-daro in the Indus Valley in the north-west of India, and all around me lay the houses and streets of this ancient city that is said to have existed over five thousand years ago; and even then it was an old and well-developed civilisation. 'The Indus civilisation,' writes Professor Childe, 'represents a very perfect adjustment of human life to a specific environment that can only have resulted from years of patient effort. And it has endured; it is already specifically Indian and forms the basis of modern Indian culture.' Astonishing thought: that any culture or civilization should have this continuity for five or six thousand years or more; and not in a static, unchanging sense, for India was changing and progressing all the time. She was coming into intimate contact with the Persians, the Egyptians, the Greeks, the Chinese, the Arabs, the Central Asians, and the peoples of the Mediterranean. But though she influenced them and was influenced by them, her cultural basis was strong enough to endure. What was the secret of this strength? Where did it come from?

I read her history and read also a part of her abundant ancient literature, and was powerfully impressed by the vigour of the thought, the clarity of the language, and the richness of the mind that lay behind it. I journeyed through India in the company of mighty travellers from China and Western and Central Asia who came here in the remote past and left records of their travels. I thought of what India had accomplished in Eastern Asia, in Angkor, Borobudur, and many other places. I wandered over the Himalayas, which are closely connected with old myth and legend, and which have influenced so much our thought and literature. My love of the mountains and my kinship with Kashmir especially drew me to them, and I saw there not only the life and vigour and beauty of the present, but also the memoried loveliness of ages past. The mighty rivers of India that flow from this great mountain barrier into the plains of India attracted me and reminded me of innumerable phases of our history. The Indus or Sindhu, from which our country came to be called India and Hindustan, and across which races and tribes and caravans and armies have come for thousands of years; the Brahmaputra, rather cut off from the main current of history, but living in old story, forcing its way into India through deep chasms cut in the heart of the northeastern mountains, and then flowing calmly in a gracious sweep between mountain and wooded plain; the Jumna, round which cluster so many legends of dance and fun and play; the Ganges, above all the river of India, which has held India's heart captive and drawn uncounted millions to her banks since the dawn of history. The story of the Ganges, from her source to the sea, from old times to new, is the story of India's civilisation and culture, of the rise and fall of empires, of great and proud cities, of the adventure of man and the quest of the mind which has so occupied India's thinkers, of the richness and fulfilment of life as well as its denial and renunciation, of ups and downs, of growth and decay, of life and death.

I visited old monuments and ruins and ancient sculptures and frescoes - Ajanta, Ellora, the Elephanta Caves, and other places - and I also saw the lovely buildings of a later age in

Agra and Delhi, where every stone told its story of India's past.

In my own city of Allahabad or in Hardwar I would go to the great bathing festivals, the *Kumbh Mela*, and see hundreds of thousands of people come, as their forebears had come for thousands of years from all over India, to bathe in the Ganges. I would remember descriptions of these festivals written thirteen hundred years ago by Chinese pilgrims and others, and even then these *melas* were ancient and lost in an unknown antiquity. What was the tremendous faith, I wondered, that had drawn our people for untold generations to this famous river of India?

These journeys and visits of mine, with the background of my reading, gave me an insight into the past. To a somewhat bare intellectual understanding was added an emotional appreciation, and gradually a sense of reality began to creep into my mental picture of India, and the land of my forefathers became peopled with living beings, who laughed and wept, loved and suffered; and among them were men who seemed to know life and understand it, and out of their wisdom they had built a structure which gave India a cultural stability which lasted for thousands of years. Hundreds of vivid pictures of this past filled my mind, and they would stand out as soon as I visited a particular place associated with them. At Sarnath, near Benares, I would almost see the Buddha preaching his first sermon, and some of his recorded words would come like a distant echo to me through two thousand five hundred years. Ashoka's pillars of stone with their inscriptions would speak to me in their magnificent language and tell me of a man who, though an emperor, was greater than any king or emperor. At Fatehpur-Sikri, Akbar, forgetful of his empire, was seated holding converse and debate with the learned of all faiths, curious to learn something new and seeking an answer to the eternal problem of man.

Thus slowly the long panorama of India's history unfolded itself before me, with its ups and downs, its triumphs and defeats. There seemed to me something unique about the continuity of a cultural tradition through five thousand years of history, of invasion and upheaval, a tradition which was widespread among the masses and powerfully influenced them. Only China has had such a continuity of tradition and cultural life. And this panorama of the past gradually merged into the unhappy present, when India, for all her past greatness and stability, was a slave country, an appendage of Britain, and all over the world terrible and devastating war was raging and brutalising humanity. But that vision of five thousand years gave me a new perspective, and the burden of the present seemed to grow lighter.

The hundred and eighty years of British rule in India were just one of the unhappy interludes in her long story; she would find herself again; already the last page of this chapter was being written. The world also will survive the horror of to-day and build itself anew on fresh foundations.

Jawaharlal Nehru
The Discovery of India
Ahmadnagar Fort Prison, 1944

India: Fifty Years into the Future

FIFTY YEARS from now, of the two stock images of India, the Taj Mahal would survive but poverty and squalor would have disappeared. India would be a reasonably prosperous land, if not quite the wonder that it once was. A romantics' delusions about a country where 37 per cent of the population are condemned to degrading poverty and deprivation, and 50 per cent are illiterate?

True, the future is the product of the present, just as the present is largely a creation of the past. India's present may not encourage much hope for a more egalitarian future.

India leads the world in the number of children who are forced to work when they should really be in school, in the absolute number of illiterate, the size of the population officially estimated to be poor. Of 1000 children born, over 80 do not survive. And 50 years is a relatively short span of time in the life of a country, particularly for a civilisation whose history goes back 5000 years BC. How can a country which could not eliminate poverty, ill-health and cultural deprivation over the millennium expect to wipe out poverty, ignorance, disease and inequality 50 years from now?

Fifty years from now, India would be the single most populous nation on earth. It is projected to overtake China in the year 2040 and will account for over 1.6 billion people, some 17 per cent of the global total of 9.5 billion human beings in 2050.

Fifty years from now, India would not only be the world's most populous country, but also a predominantly young country. But would its people be capable of producing, in a competitive fashion, the goods and services required by the global market?

Half a century hence, the market would be truly global and production processes integrated across the regions of the world. Not just economists,

but the man in the street, too, would see the globe as the optimal spatial framework for efficient production. And all producers would have to compete in this global market. Would India have the qualities and the human resources to compete effectively?

India comprises 25 states, 14 of which are large enough, geographically and in terms of their number of inhabitants, to qualify as fully-fledged nations in their own right. The population of Uttar Pradesh, for example, is 139 million. Bihar has 86 million people, Maharashtra 79 million, West Bengal, Madhya Pradesh and Andhra Pradesh each over 66 million. These states are bigger than France, Germany and Italy. Even 'tiny' Kerala has 30 million people!

They speak different languages, have different customs and living standards and eat different foods. Not only are there great variations among the states, there is great diversity within each state as well, as to levels of income, educational standards, health and overall quality of life. Kerala, for example, is 100 per cent literate, its infant mortality rate is around 16 per 1000 live births (Finland holds the world record at less than two per 1000 live births) and its population growth rate is lower than that of the best regions in China. Uttar Pradesh and Rajasthan, on the other hand, have extremely low social indicators.

There is, similarly, great diversity in the level of skills and education across society. While literacy is barely 52 per cent, India has a very large pool of skilled workers, scientific and technical manpower, managers, administrators and lawyers.

India already has the expertise to build its own satellites and put them into near-earth orbits. By the turn of the century, India will have its own launch capability to put satellites into geostationary navy orbits and will not need to depend on European, American or Russian launch vehicles. Indians are among the world's best software professionals (even if quite a few of them work outside the country) and India has a few centres of world-class excellence in education. At the same time, Indian exports are predominantly labour-intensive, low-value items that take advantage of cheap unskilled or semi-skilled labour.

This diversity is a curse as well as a blessing. Over the next 50 years, while the overall skill level would shift sharply upwards, the dispersion of skill levels is likely to remain equally large. This has enormous implications for the country's ability to compete in the global market.

The present levels of unemployment and under-employment among the low-skilled workforce in Europe suggest that the structure of global production is moving to a state where it will no longer be economical for the developed world to retain low-skilled jobs. These would migrate to developing countries where low-skill wages are only a fraction of those in the developed countries.

South India as part of the cultural exchange associated with prolonged commerce between distant communities. Legend has it that one of Christ's apostles, St Thomas, came to Kerala and converted a small number of the local people to Christianity. In any case, it is a well-documented historical fact that Christianity came to Kerala before it reached Europe. Islam also came across the Arabian Sea, along with Arab traders from the region, soon after its birth in Arabia. The local Hindu community not only did not try to prevent religious conversion but regarded the new religious groups as an integral part of society.

The reason is not religious tolerance, as many assume. The Hindu is hardly tolerant - even today in rural North India, young men and women who do not observe the dictates of caste hierarchy in love and marriage are liable to be punished by death.

The key factor would appear to be the polytheism of the Hindus. There 330 million gods in the Hindu pantheon. (Hindus outnumbered their gods for the first time early this century). So the Hindu has been inured in a tradition that respects other native paths to Godhood. The recent efforts of parties that champion Hindutva to homogenise the Hindu religion on the lines of other monotheistic religions goes against the grain of traditional culture and is more likely than not to fail. A socially cohesive India that invests in its people can go nowhere except towards medium term prosperity.

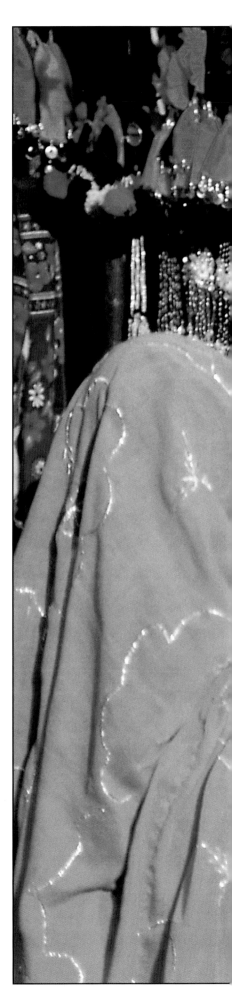

RIGHT: *A market stall in Pushkar, Rajasthan*

MONSOON *season in Mumbai. Generally starting in mid-June and petering out by mid-September, the southwest monsoon is a series of cyclones created by a cross equatorial flow from the south Indian Ocean mixing with cooler air over the Arabian Sea and the hot, continental air of Rajasthan and further west.*

A Tale of Three Cities

Mumbai, Calcutta and Delhi

Although some Indian cities, such as Benares and Puri, go back several millennia, the major cities of contemporary India are essentially colonial creations. The cities of ancient India grew largely around religious centres. In mediaeval times seats of military and political authority gradually developed into large cities and their growth and decline depended on the fate of the ruling dynasties. The arrival of the British marked the birth of another kind of city whose foundation was based on finance and commerce.

The three major coastal cities of Mumbai (formerly Bombay), Chennai (formerly Madras) and Calcutta were created to serve as channels of economic activity. Since they were centres of trade and finance, they had to be well protected, and hence Calcutta and Chennai also served as large fortified garrisons. It made sense to the British to have their seat of political authority in a prosperous and well-protected zone. So, Calcutta, which had its humble beginning in three villages in the seventeenth century, became the capital of British India.

Each of the three big cities has its unrivalled niche. During the early days of British colonialism, Calcutta credited itself to be the largest city east-of-Suez, until it was replaced by Mumbai. New Delhi continues to be the seat of the world's largest parliamentary democracy. By the year 2020, it is predicted, Mumbai will be the largest city in the world. The story of these cities is the story of modern India.

Bombay is a city with an identity crisis
Suketu Mehta, Mumbai, 1997

Mumbai traditionally did not have its own identity. It changed hands about a dozen times. It was created by the Portuguese, an able race of

ABOVE: *A newly wed couple in Tamil Nadu*

LEFT: *A bridegroom's procession in Delhi*

PREVIOUS PAGE LEFT: *Maharashtra women wear nine-yard long saris up to 50 inches in width. Pleats are divided in the middle and tucked into the waist at the back.*

PREVIOUS PAGE RIGHT: *Goan woman in traditional sari and child in Western clothes*

ABOVE: *Pilgrim at Pushkar peeps through a colourful 'chunari'*

RIGHT: *Meghalaya woman with a traditional necklace*

FAR RIGHT: *A Parsi bride with more conventional jewellery*

OPPOSITE: *High fashion influenced by tradition*

OPPOSITE: *A woman from the Lambada tribe of Andhra Pradesh carries water in an age-old style*

ABOVE: *Women from the Bastar tribe of Madhya Pradesh revel in bright colours, and wear short saris, sometimes just above their knees. The sari is wound tightly around the hip, taken up to the shoulder and tucked into the waist.*

RIGHT: *The Ratwa tribe dress of Gujarat*

ABOVE: *Folk art at the Crafts Museum in New Delhi*

LEFT: *A decorative square of cloth, chakla embroidery, made by a Rajput girl as part of her dowry and for display at the wedding ceremony*

BOTTOM LEFT: *A Punjab wedding party sculpture in the fantasy Rock Garden of Chandigarh. The four-acre garden was created by Nek Chand, a former construction worker and road inspector. He began the garden as a hobby, inspired by recurrent childhood dreams. His sculptures are made from a variety of materials, including porcelain, plates, pebbles, stone, pots and assorted scrap. The influence of tribal or 'adivasi' art can be seen in various rigid figures holding transfixed facial expressions.*

OPPOSITE: *Traditional Orissa wall painting, believed to be Subadhra, the sister of Lord Jagannath*

OPPOSITE: *A multi-coloured rock painting from a Buddhist 'vihara' (monastery) cave, one of twenty four at Ajanta, Maharashtra. They and the five chaityas (temples) are caves cut into a rather remote and sheer rock cliff of a deep ravine in the Waghore river. Monks used the caves for more than eight centuries, dating back to between 200 BC and 650 AD. Painters and sculptors decorated the caves, relying on oil-lamps or sunlight reflected by mirrors and pools of water. The painters primed the rock surface with a coating of a clay-based paste, before adding a finer layer of white lime. Once dry, an outline sketch in red dye (cinnabar) would precede the application of colours. These would include kaolin chalk for white, lamp soot for black or glauconite for green. Finally, the painters polished their work with a smooth stone.*

ABOVE: *A Buddha head, made of sandstone during the 'Gupta' period, which belonged to either a standing or seated figure. It typifies a special period of Buddhist imagery during the fifth and sixth centuries. The slightly raised eyebrows are typical of Mathura, Uttar Pradesh, a centre of Buddhist imagery.*

RIGHT: **SHIVA**, *standing and eight-armed, subduing a demon (daitya) with dagger drawn, is from the ninth or tenth century and probably crafted in Madhya Pradesh. The attributes associated with the right hands include a drum, trident, rosary and quiver. On the left there is a bow, a snake, and a club or spear in the lowest hand (here this is a broken segment). Such attributes evoke action, while the simplicity and calm in the face and torso reflect the figure's disposition. Similar prostrate figures holding a dagger beneath many figures are typical of medieval north India.*

PREVIOUS PAGE: **DANDIYA** *is a folk dance of Gujarat, in which a group of men vigorously dance with sticks to the pulsating rhythms of a drummer in the centre. This is one of the most popular entertainments performed during the Holi festival.*

LEFT: **OTTAM TULLAL**, *also called Seentankan Tulllal, is a much loved Keralian dance created by the Malayalam poet, Kunjan Nambiar in the 18th century. It is performed by one person, usually performed in temples and at marriage ceremonies. The dancer sings while performing intricate rhythmic patterns, relating the chosen story with hand gestures and facial expressions.*

ABOVE: *An Ottam Tullal dancer must also be an actor, who entertains the audience with a repertoire of asides, jokes, wit and even local gossip.*

LEFT: *Weaving its way through the infinite space of the nation's countryside.* **INDIAN RAILWAYS** *are the umbilical cord binding this vast country together, a mainstay of contacts between people and the principal artery of the national economy.*

NEXT PAGE: *The Panchachuli mountain of Uttar Pradesh*

INDIA is as large as Europe, and more diverse, covering 3,287,263 square kilometres. In the north it is bordered by the Himalayas, the world's highest mountain ranges. At its southern end, more than 3,000 kilometres away, the land gradually descends to the tropical Indian Ocean. India extends from the Arabian Sea in the west to the Bay of Bengal in the east. All three oceans converge on India's southernmost point, Kanyakumari.

There are three major river systems: the Indus, Ganga and Brahmaputra, fed by rainwater and glacial runoff from the Himalayas. Their network of tributaries nourish the fertile, silt-laden Indo-Gangetic Plain, one of the world's most densely populated regions.

The Vindhyas - a series of stepped hills - separate the Indo-Gangetic Plain from the Deccan Plateau in the centre, the oldest geographical region, in existence for over 500 million years. The Niligri Hills mark the southernmost part of the Decan Plateau. These converge with the Western Ghat and Eastern Ghats hill chains.

The rich diversity of climate, topography and vegetation is reflected by the indigenous and innumerable variety of flora and fauna. There are 500 species of mammals excluding the extinct Cheetah, last seen in 1948. There are 15,000 known species of plants, with vegetation ranging from dry desert scrub to Alpine meadows.

RIGHT: **VIVEKANANDA ROCK MEMORIAL** *at Kanyakumari is the southernmost point of the subcontinent. The memorial to philosopher Swami Vivekananda is on two rocky islands, 400 metres offshore. Kanyakumari is also another important destination for Hindu pilgrims.*

ABOVE: **KOVALAM BEACH**, *in the State of Kerala, is the most popular resort in south India*

OPPOSITE: **PARAMBIKULAM WILDLIFE SANCTUARY** *in Kerala at dawn*

PREVIOUS PAGE: **NANDI HILLS** *in Karnataka. The monsoon gives a surreal appearance to a forest.*

NEXT PAGE: *Sunset on a Goan beach*

ABOVE: *A boy watches as his mother de-husk rice in a West Bengal village*

OPPOSITE TOP: *A paddy field in Tamil Nadu*

OPPOSITE BOTTOM: *Paddy is dried in a village*

Andhra Pradesh

With a population of over 66 million, Andhra Pradesh is the largest State in the south. The Andhras, like many of their southern brethren, particularly the Keralians, Tamils and the people of Karnataka, are calm and psychologically well adjusted, with an intense and intelligent aversion to religious and communal bigotry. The major religious groups of India; Hindus, Muslims, Buddhists and Christians, with Sikh and Jain minorities, coexist peacefully in the State.

The State's other worthy claim to fame is that it is the home of the famous Nizams with their large palaces in Hyderabad, the capital. At the zenith of his incomparable financial and material glory, the last Nizam owned more Rolls Royces than any other individual on earth. Despite being the richest man in the world, the Nizam was a rather parsimonious chap. He wore shabby clothes, and ate sparingly, certainly not for reasons of health. The British, with their excessive fondness for feudal rulers, got on well with successive malleable Nizams. It was not only the British ruling elite which held the Nizams in high esteem; the Andhra 'royals' also had a mesmerising effect on their media, which never ceased to tell the world about the fabulous wealth of the Nizams.

While Telugu is the mother tongue of most Andhras, there is a large number of people, especially in mainly Muslim Hyderabad, which is bilingual, speaking Urdu in addition to Telugu. Curiously, even though Urdu evolved out of the Arabic-Hindi linguistic and racial melting pot in the North, especially in the old united Punjab, and it is the official language of the relatively new Pakistan, the vibrant Urdu literary, musical and cultural renaissance first flowered and still thrives in Hyderabad. Some of the finest and brightest Urdu scholars, writers, poets and singers, at home and abroad, are of Andhra origin.

Andhra has produced many distinguished scientists, jurists, politicians and philosophers.

Arunachal Pradesh

A RUNACHAL PRADESH lies in the eastern nook of India where the sun strikes its rays before illuminating the rest of the country. It stretches from the Assam plains of the mighty Brahmaputra river northward to the main crest of the eastern Himalayas, and eastward in an irregular line passing through a series of lofty peaks. Most of Arunachal Pradesh is mountainous. About two-thirds of the terrain is covered with forest, starting with the dense tropical rainforests in the foothills to alpine vegetation on the higher slopes. The State's northern boundary with Tibet is known as the McMahon Line. On the east it is bounded by Myanmar (Burma), the Indian States of Nagaland and Assam lie to the south, and Bhutan is to the west of this hilly State. The capital city is Itanagar.

According to legend the sage Parsuhuram opened a passage through the hills for the Brahmaputra river with the stroke of an axe at Brahma Kund. This is a well known pilgrimage centre in eastern Arunachal Pradesh.

The people of Arunachal Pradesh have physical affinities with the Tibetans and Burmese hill tribes. There are dozens of tribes and sub-tribes. These groups speak about 50 distinct languages and dialects and belong mostly to the Tibeto-Burmese linguistic family. Outsiders communicate in Assamese, Hindi or English.

The people do not intermarry, and each tribe follows distinct social, cultural and religious practices. Gods of nature and various spirits are worshipped. Ritual sacrifice is also common and the wild ox called 'mithun' is revered as a sacrificial animal. Hindu beliefs and practices have filtered into the lives of the people near the Assam lowlands. Tibetan Buddhism is practised among the tribes near the Tibetan border, and some tribes along the Myanmar border are followers of the Hinayana sect of Buddhism.

Shifting cultivation is traditional. Some tribes supplement their diet by

PREVIOUS PAGE: *A typical lowland village in Arunachal Pradesh*

OPPOSITE: *Apitani tribal woman at the handloom, an important cottage industry*

ARUNACHAL PRADESH

The 'land of the rising sun' formerly known as the North East Frontier Agency (NEFA). Its terrain is mainly wild mountainous tract along the eastern Himalayas, and it has a population of more than 20 major tribal peoples making it one of the most multicultural and multilingual regions in the world.

Population*	864,600
Area	83, 743 sq. km.
Population Density (per sq. km.)*	10
Population Growth (1981-1991)	36.8%
Principal Languages	Adi, Alka, Dafla, Gallong, Miji, Mishmi, Monpa, Nishi, Nocte, Tagin Hill, Miri, Tangsa and Wancho
Capital	Itanagar
Date of Statehood	February 20, 1987

Seats in Parliament - *Rajya Sabha:Lok Sabha*   1:2
* based on 1991 Census

Agriculture:

Shifting cultivation (Jhum). Forests cleared for crops for one to three years depending on soil fertility. Provides a livelihood for 35% of the population. 17% of the total cultivated area is irrigated. Principal crops are rice, maize, millet, wheat, potato, sugarcane and mustard. 62% of the total area is under forest.

Industry:

Forest and wood products, cottage industries such as handloom and handicrafts, pottery, soap and candle-making. Mineral reserves include coal, crude oil, dolomite, limestone, graphite, quartzite, kyanite, mica, iron and copper ore.

hunting, fishing and gathering forest products. Settled agriculture is practised on less than half the arable land.

The tribal people have a glorious arts and crafts heritage. They take immense pride in their colourful apparel, and each group sport distinctive garments and headdress. They are highly accomplished in the art of weaving and their textile designs are of a rare beauty.

The people are undemanding and hospitable, jealous of their way of life. Colourful festivals reflect their faith in the power of nature. Dancing and chorus songs are an integral part of community life. Each tribal group has its own festival which is celebrated with ebullience.

Arunachal Pradesh has a wide profusion of flora and fauna, including a veritable treasure trove of orchid wealth. The lush forests are home to more than 650 varieties of this exotic flower. An Orchid Research and Development Centre has been established and researchers are still identifying new varieties. Their flowering season is from April to November.

The State has a number of wildlife sanctuaries and national parks. The musk deer and takin are rare species still found in the wild. Namdhapa National Park has the unique distinction of housing four of the cat family, the tiger, leopard, snow leopard and clouded leopard.

Assam

ASSAM is associated with tea, oilfields, earthquakes, elephants and rhinos, the mighty Brahmaputra river and a charming and friendly people. The State is India's doorway to South-East Asia, and bears the imprint of the latter's culture.

Over the past five decades Assam has often been turbulent. The main ethnic group are the Ahom. But they have never been so numerous as to fully prevail over other ethnic groups. Ethnic differences in the Mongoloid-dominated north-eastern India have fostered separatism. Since 1947, the States of Meghalaya (Khasi-Jayanti tribes), Nagaland (Angami-Ao and other tribes), and Mizoram (Lushai tribe), Manipur (Meitei) and Arunachal Pradesh (Dafla and other tribes) have been carved out of old Assam.

The Government of India blames foreign forces for promoting violent conflict in Assam and throughout the region. The State has lived with the challenge of instability for the last three decades.

Large numbers of farm workers from what is now Bangladesh were encouraged by the British, and later by some Indian politicians in the State, to emigrate to the sparsely-populated Assam to clear forests and grow certain crops. This too has become a source of communal tension. All these factors have served to hold back Assam's development.

Tea, timber and petroleum are largely controlled by non-locals. The impoverished indigenous peoples of Assam feel they are getting a raw deal. Poor communications have been a problem, but with promises of improvement the Assamese economy may take off. Among the State's greatest assets are its flora and fauna. Tourism, very promising a few decades ago, has yet to realise its full potential. A more stable Assam however, will attract environmental enthusiasts to the world famous Kaziranga National Park, home of the great one-horned rhino, native to the country.

The beautiful Bihu dance is one of the very pleasant features of the

State's harvest festival. While daily life in Assam is unhurried, and its patient and stoic people have refused to be intimidated or cowed, it seems they will have to wait for an end to conflict before they can reap the rewards they so richly deserve from tourism and their State's abundant natural resources.

ABOVE: *A memorial to Gandhi stands on Kamyakha Hill in Gaumati*

PREVIOUS PAGE: *The Brahmaputra river in Assam*

OPPOSITE: *A tea-picker at work in Assam which produces 60 per cent of the country's tea*

ASSAM

After Independence, a northern section was ceded to Bhutan (1951), the Naga Hill District became part of Nagaland in 1962, the districts of Garo Hills, Khasi and Jaitia Hills became the State of Meghalaya in 1970, and the Mizo Hill district became part of the Union Territory (now State) of Mizoram in 1972.

Population*	22.4 million
Area	78, 438 sq. km.
Population Density (per sq. km.)*	286
Population Growth (1981-1991)	24.2%
Principal Languages	Assamese and Bengali
Capital	Dispur
Date of Statehood	1921
Seats in Parliament	
- *Rajya Sabha: Lok Sabha*	7:14

* based on 1991 Census

Agriculture:
70% of the population work on the land providing 50% of State revenue. 79% of the total cultivated area is used for food crops, principally rice. Major cash crops are tea, jute, cotton, mustard and rape, potato and fruits. Assam is the national leader in sugar cane production. 22% of the land is under forest.

Principal Industries:
Assam tea accounts for 16% of the entire world production and provides employment for nearly half a million people in over 800 plantations. The State produces a significant proportion of the country's total petroleum output and natural gas, with three oil refineries. Petroleum exploration continues. These are reserves of coal, limestone, refractory clay and dolomite. Petrochemicals, fertiliser, sugar refining, jute, silk, paper and paper products, rice and oil milling and handloom weaving are major growth areas.

Bihar

T HE STATE of Bihar lies on the eastern Gangetic plain in North India. Cutting across the State from west to east, the bountiful Ganga has made the region so fertile that its natural prosperity has nurtured, advanced and refined civilisations for centuries.

Bihar comprises the Chota Nagpur Plateau in the southeastern region and the middle Gangetic plain in the northern half of the State. In common with many ancient civilisations the Indian way of life was also centred around its magnificent rivers. Few rivers of the world have shaped and invigorated the culture, economy and character of the people along its banks as has the Ganga. Here, kingdom after kingdom rose and fell, leaving their indelible mark on history. Kings fought bloody battles devastating the land and people. Yet by some strange alchemy, the same land has been midwife to the birth of some gentle and progressive religious teachers like Gautama Buddha and Mahavira Jain.

The Chota Nagpur Plateau forms the northeastern part of peninsular India. Hills and ridges, winding rivers, valleys and basins characterise the region. A thick canopy of green forest also embraces placid lakes and turbulent waterfalls. This plateau is also the richest mineral belt of the entire sub-continent and contains the world's largest reserves of mica.

Bihar is the birthplace of two great religions, Buddhism and Jainism. Lord Buddha, the gentle colossus who created what is often held to be the world's first rational religion, worked and lived for much of his life in Bihar. Though the Buddha was born a Sakya prince in the Terai foothills of the Himalayas, his last and most famous and enduring sermon was delivered in Bihar. The State is home to the renowned centre of Buddhist learning, Nalanda University. This was the first residential international university in the world. Hiuen Tsang, the Chinese scholar, stayed here in the seventh century, leaving detailed descriptions of the excellence of the education and the purity of monastic life practised there. The State's name originated from 'Vihara', a term describing the Buddhist and Jain monasteries, which once flourished here.

The Chota Nagpur Plateau is an anthropologist's delight. The ancient lifestyle of the aborigines remains almost intact. Dance and song are the oxygen of life for the tribals. Their songs are generally accompanied by dances that change in harmony with the rhythms of the seasons.

The jungles of Chota Nagpur abound in wildlife. There are 14 wildlife sanctuaries and two National Parks. There are tree-top towers, watch towers and ground level hideouts for the benefit of wildlife enthusiasts. The Palamau National Park comes under the Project Tiger Programme.

Bihar is famous for its indigenous art of Madhubani paintings. Originally humble representations of the creativity of rural women, village wall paintings now adorn many city homes. This art, peculiar to the genius of the women of Mithila, in primary colours of natural origin on paper and cloth, narrates mythological and religious events.

PREVIOUS PAGE: **SONEPUR MELA** *in Bihar is held over two weeks, determined by the full moon in the Hindu month of Karttika (October/November). This is considered the most auspicious time to bathe on the right bank of the river Gandak, near the confluence with the Ganga. In a thousand-year long struggle between Gaj the elephant, Lord of the Forest, and Garah the crocodile, Lord of Water, the elephant triumphed with the help of Hari, the Supreme God. Elephants also enjoy a dip in the river. The Sonepur Mela, with its sale of elephants, cattle, camels, horses and other animals is believed to be the largest in Asia.*

BIHAR

Home of the Mauryan Emperors with its famous capital of Pataliputra in the reign of Ashoka. Its name is associated with 'vihara', a monastery or centre of learning.

Population*	87 million
Area	173, 877 sq. km.
Population Density (per sq. km.)*	497
Population Growth (1981-1991)	23.5%
Principal Language	Hindi
Capital	Patna
Date of Statehood	1936
Seats in Parliament - *Rajya Sabha: Lok Sabha*	22:54

* based on 1991 Census

Agriculture:
82% of the population work on the land. 35% of cultivable land is under irrigation. Rice, wheat, maize, ragi and pulses are the main food crops. Sugarcane, oilseeds, tobacco, potato and jute are major cash crops. Around 16% of the land is under forest.

Industry:

The State produces 40% of the country's entire mineral production and it has generous deposits of copper, apatatite, kyanite, coal, mica and china clay, iron ore, manganese, limestone, graphite, asbestos, barytes, dolomite, felspar, slate, lead and silver. Manufacturing includes iron, steel, aluminum and associated products, heavy engineering (vehicles, diesel engines, railway wagons, machine tools) and handicrafts.

ABOVE: *Chilli pepper is one of the main cash crops of Bihar*

Goa

GOA, a former Portuguese colony, is famous for its silvery sands and seemingly endless coastline. The State nestles in the creek of the Sahyadri Ranges and coconut groves gloriously stretch as far as the eye can see. With its unique heritage, Goa, sandwiched between the Arabian Sea and the Western Ghats, still retains its Portuguese cultural flavour.

Predominant Deccan influence blends harmoniously with Hindu and Muslim cultures. Before the arrival of the Portuguese, Goa was a part of several empires.

Goa is derived from the local language, Konkani. 'Goyan' means a patch of tall grass. The State's origin is ascribed to Parshuram, a God of the Hindu pantheon. This mythical land was known in Sanskrit as 'Aparanto', meaning a place in the sun, unfettered by time. The Portuguese came to trade in silk and spices but settled down, mixed with the local inhabitants and made this paradise on earth their home.

The 451 years of Portuguese colonial rule have left their social, religious and cultural imprint. Goan weddings, which combine Catholic and Indian traditions, are celebrated with dancing and singing. The feast day of the patron saint is a major event, for which whole villages turn out. Hindu festivals call for colourful processions. Even in between feasts and festivals, the irrepressible Goans cannot resist revelry.

The strip of land on the Malabar coast has a 100-kilometres long coastline, home to some of the world's most beautiful beaches. Uninterrupted white sand with swaying palms and turquoise waters, exude an aura of sublime peace and tranquillity. The entire coastline is dotted with an assortment of hotels and eating places. The architecture, from old style Portuguese to modern, is part of Goa's unique charm. Some of the beaches were once the haunt of 'flower children' and still retain the liberated ambience of those days. Many of the beaches have well-developed resorts, with luxury hotels serving gourmet meals.

Goa is famous for its tasty seafood and excellent wines. While the

GOA

The 25th and smallest of the Indian States, it was a former Portuguese settlement together with Daman, Diu, Dadra and Nagar Haveli. Goa became an administered territory in 1961 when India regained control of the State.

Population*	1.2 million
Area	3, 702 sq. km.
Population Density (per sq. km.)*	316
Population Growth (1981-1991)	16.1%
Principal Language	Konkani and Marathi
Capital	Panaji
Major ports	Panaji,
	Momugao (cargo)
Date of Statehood	May 30, 1987
Seats in Parliament	
- Rajya Sabha: Lok Sabha	1:2

* based on 1991 Census

Agriculture:

About 9% of the cultivated area is under irrigation, with rice the principal food crop. Pulses, ragi, groundnut, maize, jowar and bajra are also grown. Principal occupation: Horticulture, with cultivation of cash crops such as coconut, pineapple, banana, mango, jackfruit and cashew.

Industry:

Of primary importance is the mining and the export of iron ore, ferromanganese, bauxite and silica sand. Fruit and fish canning, chemicals and pesticides, synthetic products and tyres, industrial gases, brewing, diamond cutting, footwear and fishing nets on a smaller scale.

ABOVE: *Bullfights in Goa are an inheritance from the Portuguese past. The bulls sometimes run amok.*

PREVIOUS PAGE: **SHIGMO** *is the Goan version of the Holi festival. There is a large parade in the capital Panaji, with more modest festivals at temples.*

RIGHT: *At a family shrine a Goan wife makes an offering for her husband's well-being*

cuisine has a mild but discernible Portuguese influence, the delicate spices and herbs of India are more dominant, producing a flavour and taste acclaimed by food lovers and critics worldwide.

The International Sea Festival in November and the Carnival in April attract huge domestic and international participation.

Gujarat

GUJARAT lies in the north-west of the country, stretching from the fertile rice-growing plains of the west coast to the salt desert of Kachchh in the northwest. The Rann of Kachchh is a vast salt marsh covering about 8,000 square miles. In the dry season it is a sandy plain plagued by dust storms. To the south of Kachchh is the large peninsular of Kathiawar, between the Gulf of Kachchh and the Gulf of Khambat. This area is also arid and rises from the coast to a low rolling hilly terrain covered with scrub or sparse woodland.

Gujarat has traded with Europe since Greco-Roman times. The first remains of the Indus Valley civilisation, dating back to 6,000 BC, have been recently excavated at Lothal in the Kathiawar peninsular. The Parsis, Zoroastrians who fled Persia sometime after the seventh century, initially settled on the coast of Gujarat, but later moved to Mumbai.

The intermingling of many invaders with the locals added to the ethnic diversity. Some are Indic, with a strong northern influence, others Dravidian, with southern characteristics. Some tribes are a mixture of the two. Gujarat owes its name to the Gurjars, a subtribe of the Huns who ruled during the eighth and ninth centuries. Because of the State's trading heritage, the Gujarati language employs many Farsi, Arabic, Turkish, Portuguese and English words. It is an Indo-European language, derived from Sanskrit through Prakrit, an ancient Indian language, and Apabhramsha, a language spoken in northern and western India from between the tenth and fourteenth centuries.

Gujaratis are mainly Hindus with Jain, Muslim and Zoroastrian minorities. Mahatma Gandhi was born in Gujarat and he built his ashram on the banks of the Sabarmati.

Folklore is inspired by the mythology surrounding the Hindu deity Krishna in the Puranas. The rasnritya and raslila dances in honour of Lord Krishna have survived in the form of a popular folk dance, the garba, performed at the nine day Narvaratri festival, where men and women move in a circle, singing, clapping and dancing. Another popular

Himachal Pradesh

HIMACHAL PRADESH is almost entirely mountainous. Himachal means 'snow mountain', the State taking its name from the majestic Himalayas. The terrain varies, with its mountain peaks, thickly forested hills, wooded valleys, passing into virgin country and fast flowing rivers. Prominent mountains which rise to about 22,000 feet are the Himalayan ranges of the Pir Panjal, Hathi and Dhauladhar. These are popular resort towns, with mighty mountain ranges forming the border with Tibet.

The history of Himachal Pradesh goes back to *Vedic* times. This region was also invaded over the centuries but each wave of newcomers met with the quintessentially Indian process of absorption. The State is one of the least urbanised in India. Hill tribes and recent immigrants compete with each other for the soil. The majority are Hindus, except in Lahaul and Spiti, where Buddhism is the main religion. With more than 60 dialects, the State's main language is Pahari, a derivation from Sanskrit and Prakrit. The people appear to be indifferent to what they consider alien notions of progress.

The ancient Hindus regarded Himachal Pradesh as the English equivalent of 'world's end'. The epics claim its people divinely inspired musicians and singers. More than a hundred festivals are celebrated in a year, interspersed with local fairs. These are occasions to dress in rich brocades and exquisitely embroidered silk. Masked performers do devil dances depicting the victory of good over evil.

The hill tribes are used to isolation. More cut off from the outside world due to bad weather, each tribe has a distinct social and cultural life that is preserved zealously. Malana, in the Kulu district is reputed to be the oldest democracy in the world, with all the inhabitants of the village involved in its affairs. The people of Kinnaur practice polyandry.

The region is famous for its art and craft. The Kangra Valley school of

paintings is appreciated the world over. Exquisitely designed shawls of Kinnaur, the distinctive woollen caps of Kullu, and the embroidered scarves of Chamba accent their colourful festive clothing. The old Hindustan-Tibet road, which was the main trade route to and from Tibet, passes through the Kinnaur valley. A walk down what remains of this road is fascinating.

Simla, the capital of this beautiful State was also the summer capital of the British Raj. It still holds lingering echoes of its colonial past with its neo-Gothic churches and Viceregal lodge. At Dharamsala, the whirring sounds of Tibetan prayer wheels greet you. It is here, in McLeodganj, that the Dalai Lama resides. The monastery and the School of Tibetan Studies are among the best places to learn about Tibetan culture. The Kulu valley is known as the 'Valley of the Gods'. The colourful Dussehra festival is held here every autumn. Nearly two hundred Gods from across the valley descend in their chariots to pay homage to the presiding deity in Kulu.

HIMACHAL PRADESH

Himachal means 'Lap of Snow'. The State is made up of 30 former Punjab hill states in the foothills of the Himalayas.

Population*	5.1 million
Area	55, 673m sq. km.
Population Density (per sq. km.)*	93
Population Growth (1981-1991)	20.8%
Principal languages	Hindi and Pahari
Capital	Simla
Date of Statehood	January 25, 1971
Seats in Parliament	
- *Rajya Sabha: Lok Sabha*	3:4

* based on 1991 Census

LEFT: **KALACHARA FESTIVAL** *draws a large number of Buddhist devotees who come to partake of food blessed by the Dalai Lama*

PREVIOUS PAGE: *The remote Ki Buddhist monastery*

ABOVE: *Naga tribal woman works with a handloom*

Agriculture:
75% of the population produce nuts, and cash crops such as sugarcane, potato, ginger and olive are an important source of State revenue. The main food crops are wheat, maize, rice, barley, rice. Forests occupy 68% of the land.

Industry:
Mineral reserves include rock salt, gypsum, limestone and barytes. Resin and turpentine, brewing, fertiliser, cement, watch and watch parts also provide employment and revenue, as does tourism. The town of Pawanoo has the largest fruit processing plant in Asia.

Jammu & Kashmir

J AMMU & KASHMIR, India's captivating northernmost State, comprises three distinctive regions differing widely in topography and culture. Jammu, on the foothills, was the stronghold of the Hindu Dogra kings. Predominantly Muslim in character, Kashmir nestles in the Himalayas. Ladakh is a vast expanse of high altitude desert inhabited mainly by Buddhists.

Jammu on the low lying foothills of the Himalayas, is the most varied of the three regions. There is much natural beauty in its forest clad hills, and also barren terrain as the mountains give way to the plains. Everywhere in the city, spires of temples reach out to the sky, earning it the title of 'Temple City'. Jammu is also the winter capital of the State as the seat of government moves to the plains when Srinagar, in the Kashmir valley, is freezing and snowbound.

Set like a jewelled crown, Kashmir is a many faceted diamond changing its character with the seasons. Three Himalayan ranges, Karakoram, Pir Panjar and Zanskar, frame the landscape from northwest to northeast. These snow-capped mountains are the origins of the great rivers that flow down into the valleys, forested with wild orchards and lily-laden lakes. Kashmir has within its territories, all the elements of nature at its best, with a stunning profusion of colour. Legend has it that the Kashmir valley was once a lake as large as a sea where lived a demon which was killed by the Goddess Parvati.

Ladakh means 'the land of passes'. It is located between the two highest mountain ranges in the world, the South Himalayas and the North Karakoram. A maze of enormously high snow-capped peaks and the largest glaciers outside the polar region dominate the terrain. Valley heights range from 8,000 feet to 15,000 feet, with passes of up to 20,000 feet and peaks

Karnataka

INDEPENDENT India's thrust to modernisation is perhaps most imaginatively reflected in Bangalore. In their drive to industrialisation, the planners found the older seaboard cities, dominated by colonial industries, congested and in decline. Bangalore, which had in place the infrastructure for modern industry before independence, proved an ideal location.

The Indian Institute of Science, one of the country's foremost centres of excellence, was established as far back as 1912 - born out of the convergence of interests between the ruler of the erstwhile princely State of Mysore (precursor of modern-day Karnataka), and the rising industrial house of the Tatas.

Where other cities were seeking to rid themselves of the detritus of their obsolete colonial industries, Bangalore moved swiftly into the realm of electronics, communications and aviation. When the information age dawned in the 1970s, Bangalore was the springboard for a leap into the future.

Bangalore figures prominently on the radar screen of every major investor in information technology. This is due as much to its infrastructural endowment as its highly prized human resources.

The new generation of information age professionals are the most visible community in Bangalore. In its rapid growth and modernity, the city mirrors the lifestyle of this assertive new class.

Inevitably, the tensions of rapid modernisation are apparent in Bangalore. No other State capital in India represents such a linguistic mélange as Bangalore, with the local language, Kannada, restricted to a minority of the city's residents.

However, Kannada is not only alive but in robust good health in its literal form. No other regional literature presents such sensitive and perceptive analysis of the encounter between tradition and modernity. This is a major preoccupation of modern Kannada literature and of its drama, which has been superbly translated into film.

The best of Kannada literature and art is not simply centred around the consequence of modernity. Their clearest articulation is to be found in the older, but smaller cities of Mysore, Hubli-Dharwar and Shimoga. These are the pioneer revivers of traditional art forms and are also known for their interpretations in contemporary settings.

LEFT: *The neo-Gothic St. Philomena's Cathedral in Mysore took eight years to build, 1933-1941, and is one of the largest churches in India*

PREVIOUS PAGE: **BANGALORE**, *the capital city of Karnataka, is one of the fastest growing cities in Asia and an important industrial centre, dubbed the 'Silicon Valley of India'. The city's confidence is reflected in the high quality of its educational institutions and the sophisticated skills of its workforce, evoking this tribute from computer supremo, Bill Gates: "After the Chinese, the South Indians are the cleverest people in the world". Modern, 'hi-tech' industries and multinational corporations are finding the city's growing cosmopolitan, cultural and progressive milieu much to their liking.*

RIGHT: **A DWAR PALAKA**, *guardian of the door*

KARNATAKA

'Karunadu' lofty land, the southern capital of the ancient Mauryan Kingdom. The first State to have generated electricity (1887). The 'Silicon Valley of India'.

Population*	44.8 million
Area	191, 791 sq. km.
Population Density (per sq. km.)*	960
Population Growth (1981-1991)	21.1%
Principal language	Kannada
Capital	Bangalore
Major port	New Mangalore
Date of Statehood	Originally as Mysore, November 1, 1956 and renamed in 1973
Seats in Parliament - *Rajya Sabha: Lok Sabha*	12:28

* based on 1991 Census

Agriculture:
Provides work for 65% of the population and generates nearly 50% of the State's income. Leading producer of coffee and ragi. Food crops include rice, wheat, milletts and pulses. Sugarcane, cardamom, arecanut, coconut, groundnut, jowar, cotton, mulberry, tobacco, cashew, pepper, oranges, grapes and oilseeds are the principal cash crops. Forests occupy 20% of the total area.

Industry:
Rich deposits of high-grade iron ore, manganese ore, limestone, china clay, asbestos, corundum, felspar and quartz. It is the only State where gold and chromite are mined for export. Large scale manufacturing includes machine tools, aircraft, electrical goods and telecommunications equipment, watches, sugar refining, chemical and pharmaceutical goods, cement, ceramics and porcelain. The State produces 85% of the country's raw silk, its sandal soap and oil are world renowned. Karnataka is a leading producer of electronic equipment.

Kerala

THE STATE is best known for its 100 per cent literacy rate and the disproportionately large number of its sons and daughters who have enriched the nation's intelligentsia, politics, diplomacy, science and technology and even the security service. Indeed, the mastermind behind the modern Indian security apparatus is a Keralian who testifies to an astonishingly high level of political maturity.

Kerala has in place a social welfare system that challenges the conventional wisdom, notably the assumption that improvements in social standards should follow, rather than precede or accompany, the growth of industry. The Kerala model offers rich material for social scientists studying the dynamics of modern development processes.

The Malayali (as Keralites are more correctly known) are a ubiquitous presence across the country, well entrenched in the trades and professions. A steady trickle of Malayali guest workers to the oil producing nations of western Asia in earlier years, became a torrent in the 1970s. The earnings of the Malayali diaspora in western Asia have underwritten a substantial part of Kerala's economic and social development targets.

Kerala, "God's own country", is a compact region of great ecological diversity, bounded on the west by a mountain range and on the east by the ocean. Kerala's short width is punctuated by a number of west flowing rivers which drain into large inland lakes. Fringed by coconut palms, these lakes are the jewel in the crown of the State's flourishing tourism industry. There are striking topographic contrasts, from the placid inland waters to the untouched tropical forest with a maze of rivers.

Situated on the western seaboard of the sub-continent, enriched by early cultural relations with Europe and the Arab lands, Kerala, has a cosmopolitan mix of cultures like few other States of India. The State is a model of cultural tolerance and peaceful coexistence through honest power sharing arrangements.

A cause and consequence of the high level of literacy in the State is the intense popular involvement in the political process. Impassioned political

OPPOSITE: **POORAM** *is Kerala's principal festival and is held in the Hindu month of Vaisakhi (April/May). It is one of the biggest in the south and is celebrated in Trichur. Introduced by the maharajah of the former State of Kochi, Skathan Thampuram, the highlights are brightly decorated, caparisoned elephants, colourful processions and a dazzling display of fireworks.*

debate on local, national or international issues is at an informed and critical level. Malayalam newspapers are among the largest circulated in the country.

Scores of thousands of Malayalis live in economic exile. Nostalgia for home has never quite impeded this easy adaptability to a variety of milieux, though the insistence on an emotional bulwark of close associates from one's own State often mitigates the pain of separation.

Probably Kerala's greatest historian, one of world stature, was K. M. Pannikar, who was also an ace diplomat. Kerala has been home to many other famous sons and daughters of India, including Krishna Menon, a former Foreign Minister and leader of the Indian delegation at the United Nations, V. P. S. Menon, the man who brought the princely States into line after independence, Mrs Lakshimi Menon, Deputy Foreign Minister in the first Nehru government, and E. M. S. Namboodripad, acknowledged as one of the world's leading Marxist theoreticians.

OPPOSITE ABOVE: **ONAM SNAKE-BOAT RACE** *in Aranmula, Kerala, is a harvest celebration at the close of the south-west monsoon season. The festival is a loving welcome for the benevolent Malayalam King, Mahabali, who is believed to return to the kingdom once a year. In preparation for his arrival, houses are cleaned, streets are decorated with flowers and feasts are held. The boats are of various shapes, decorated with green and scarlet silk umbrellas, and adorned with gold coins and tassels. The sound of drums and cymbals pour out of every boat during the race.*

OPPOSITE BELOW: **BACKWATERS** *of Kerala are a picturesque and unique network of rivers, canals, lakes and lagoons penetrating far inland from the Arabian Sea, between Alappuzha (Allepey) and Kollam (Quillon). The region's friendly and distinct lifestyle lures thousands of tourists from Europe and North America. The palm-fringed lakes are rich in fish caught by fishermen using cantilevered Chinese nets. Barges transport coconut fibre (coir), dried coconut meat (copra) and cashew along shaded canals. Boats with large sails and prows serenely glide along the wider canals and lagoons.*

KERALA

The 'land of Green Magic', the subcontinent's most southern point at Kanniyakumari. Its famous and enchanting 'backwaters' are a vital part of Kerala's economy, especially for transport, tourism and communications. The State is the first in India to claim 100% literacy.

Population*	29 million
Area	38, 863 sq. km.
Population Density (per sq. km.)*	749
Population Growth (1981-1991)	14.3%
Principal Language	Malayalam
Capital	Thiruvananthapuram
Major port	Kochi
Date of Statehood	November 1, 1956
Seats in Parliament - *Rajya Sabha: Lok Sabha*	9:20

* based on 1991 Census

Agriculture:
53% of the population is involved. 13% of the cultivated land is under irrigation. There is an abundance of cash crops including coconut, cashew, oilseeds, pepper, sugarcane, rubber, tea, coffee, cardamom, pulses, banana, pineapple, jackfruit, ginger and spices such as nutmeg, cinnamon and cloves. Rice and tapioca are the important foodgrain crops. Forests cover 24% of the land.

Principal Industries:
The beach sands contain valuable minerals, ilmenite, rutile, quartz, zircon and sillimanite. There are also white clay deposits, mica, limestone, lignite, plus graphite and kaolin. Exports include rare earths, and tile and bricks, porcelain, cement, rubber, chemicals, paper and printing, shark-liver oil, rayon, timber (teak, ebony, rosewood and sandalwood included) and coir. Kerala also has India's largest fishing industry.

Madhya Pradesh

BHOPAL, the State's capital, is indelibly associated with the terrible Union Carbide tragedy which virtually poisoned the entire town, claiming hundreds of lives and leaving thousands permanently disabled. Such was the scale and depth of the explosion, triggered off by lax safety standards, which reflected badly both on Union Caribide and on the State and central government, that the atmosphere is still not completely free of poison gases.

The people of Madhya Pradesh, proud, sensitive and defiant, have throughout their long and brave history never surrendered to any form of tyranny or repression from however powerful a quarter, be it British or Mughal. Madhya Pradesh also gave its grandest manhood to the struggle against British rule, both the violent and the non-violent versions.

Even the *Dacoits*, bandits and robbers, have been endowed with a typically Madhya Pradesh social conscience. When the Mughals came down hard on them, the Dacoits took to the hills in classical guerrilla fashion and ran rings around their opponents who were eventually forced to retreat. The British never entirely succeeded in their many 'programmes' of repression against the revolutionary and rebellious people of Madhya Pradesh.

Gwalior, the capital, is also the seat of the great Nawabs of Pataudi, one of them,"Tiger" Pataudi, captaining the Indian national cricket Test side in the 60s.

There were some powerful Maharajahs too, among them the Scindias. Maharania Scindia founded the eponymous shipping line, one of the largest carriers in the world, competing at its peak with the likes of Aristotle Onasis and other Greek giants. Maharani Scindia is probably the world's first and only woman at the helm of a major shipping company, her achievement being even more remarkable considering her enterprise's remarkable capacity and efficiency.

PREVIOUS PAGE: **THE TEMPLES AT KHAJURAHO**, *originating in the 10th century, are an outstanding example of Indo-Aryan architecture from the Chandela dynasty. The temples are equally well known for their erotic figures (mithuna). Every March there is a ten-day dance festival with performances by some of the country's top classical dancers.*

LEFT: **GWALIOR**, *a legendary hilltop fortress, dominates the town ninety metres below. The fortress was built during the first century and is a major tourist attraction, along with local hobby horse dancers and drummers.*

MADHYA PRADESH

The largest State, formerly the Central Province.

Population*	66.2 million
Area	443, 446 sq. km.
Population Density (per sq. km.)*	149
Population Growth (1981-1991)	26.8%
Principal language	Hindi
Capital	Bhopal
Date of Statehood	November 1, 1956
Seats in Parliament - *Rajya Sabha: Lok Sabha*	16:40

* based on 1991 Census

Agriculture:
45% of the land is cultivable, of which 18% is under irrigation. 80% of the population live in villages and work in agriculture. The main food crops are jowar, rice, wheat and gram. Sugarcane, groundnut, linseed, mustard and rape, castor, tobacco and cotton are the main cash crops. Forest covers 32% of the land.

Industry:
Mineral deposits include coal, iron ore, bauxite, manganese ore, limestone, clay, dolomite, marble, corundum, asbestos, shales, silica, graphite and mica copper. Madhya Pradesh is the only producer of diamonds and tin ore. Other industries include steel and steel casting, engineering tools, paper and pulp, potteries, industrial gases, solvent extraction, telecommunication products such as optical fibre, engineering tools and products, and textiles - rayon and art silk. Synthetics and drugs are major industries. The State is the leading producer of cement. Its handloom weaving centres in Chanderi and Maheshware are noted for their skills and quality.

Maharashtra

MAHARASHTRA, the land of the Marathas, who produced some of India's greatest warriors, occupies a substantial part of the Deccan Plateau in the western peninsula. The central Indian tableland merges with undulating hill ranges, which in turn merge with the majestic Western Ghats before serenely descending to palm-fringed beaches. Military forts and fortifications remind us of an incredibly brave soldiery, who destroyed the Mughals and nearly did the same to the British Raj. Lowland temples bear the imprint of the Marathas' artistic, architectural and sculptural skills. Mumbai (formerly Bombay), one of the world's most cosmopolitan cities, is its capital.

Maharashtra resembles a triangle with a long western coastline at the base, and the eastern interior narrowing to a blunt apex some 500 miles away. To the extreme west is the narrow Konkan coastal lowland, which is widest near Mumbai. Minor hills dominate. Small, swift streams flow west into the Arabian Sea. The Western Ghats, a mountain range at the western edge of the Deccan Plateau, run north-south, its foothills reaching to within four miles of the Arabian Sea. Roads and rail link the coast to the interior. The eastern slopes of the Ghats descend gently to the Deccan Plateau, with the wide, fertile valleys of the major rivers of south India adding to the scenic splendour.

The Marathas are India's last great conquering people. The near impregnable forts which still survive were the work of the mighty Sluvaji, the Maratha leader who restored large parts of north India to Indian rule.

Tribal peoples resembling the Aborigines of Australia coexist with the Kumbi Marathas, descendants of settlers who came from the north around the beginning of the first century AD. The aboriginals and immigrants mixed freely.

Hindus predominate, followed by Muslims and Buddhists. Other religious minorities live in peaceful coexistence. The Parsis, who fled Iran, took refuge in this State in the seventh century. Mumbai, together with Cochin and Calcutta, is one of the few places in the world where the Jews were never persecuted.

Literature played an important role in unifying the Marathas. This was further strengthened by its classical and devotional music, and the Marathi theatre. *Tamasha* - music, drama and dance - are much loved in the countryside. A typical tamasha troupe comprises seven artists, including a female dancer and a bawdy clown.

The *Ganesh Chaturthi* festival during the rainy season is by far the most popular. Everyone joins the procession while songs and traditional dances enliven the fun. *Dusschra*, an autumn festival commemorates the day on which the Maratha warriors started their military campaigns.

LEFT: **GREAT CHAITYA CAVE** *is the largest of 109 Kanheri Caves on Elephanta Island, in the Sanjay Gandhi National Park near Mumbai. The caves housed monasteries (viharas) or temples (chaityas) used by Buddhist monks between the 2nd and 9th centuries.*

ABOVE: *A petrochemical complex in Jalgaon, one of highly-industrialised Maharashtra's giants*

PREVIOUS PAGE: *The spectacular Marine Drive in Mumbai*

MAHARASHTRA

Formerly Bombay State, its northern and western Gujarati-speaking districts are now a separate State.

Population *	79 million
Area	307, 713 sq. km.
Population Density (per sq. km.) *	257
Population Growth (1981-1991)	25.7%
Principal Language	Marathi
Capital	Mumbai
Major ports	Mumbai and Nhave Sheva
Year of Statehood	May 1, 1960
Seats in Parliament - *Rajya Sabha: Lok Sabha*	19:48

* *based on 1991 Census*

Agriculture:
70% of the population cultivate 60% of the land. Only 12% of the cropped area is under irrigation. Food crops include rice, wheat, jowar, bajra and pulses. Oilseeds, sugarcane and cotton, groundnut and tobacco are the primary cash crops. Forest covers 27% of the State's total land area.

Industry:
There are large mineral deposits of manganese ore, iron ore, coal, bauxite, limestone, dolomite, ilmenite, kyanite, sillimanite, clay, silica and sand. Copper, lead, zinc, tungsten, barytes, felspar, mica, asbestos, graphite and corundum are also present. Cotton textiles, ginning and pressing, silk, rayon and synthetic fabrics, general and electrical engineering, sophisticated electronic equipment, dairy and vegetable products, sugar refining and paper mills, pharmaceuticals, chemicals and petrochemicals , heavy oil refining, food processing, industrial alcohol, plastics and steel products, marine industries and fish processing add to Maharashtra's revenues. 'Bollywood' is the centre of the Indian film industry.

The North East States

Manipur • Meghalaya Mizoram • Nagaland Sikkim • Tripura

Until the 1960s, most of this region, with the exception of Sikkim, which did not formally join the Indian Union until the next decade, formed part of the single state of Assam. However, new States were successively created in order to take account of the region's diversity and to promote stability through the recognition of the unique characteristics of the various peoples. Together with Assam and Arunachal Pradesh, but excepting Sikkim, these States are often described as the 'Seven Sisters' and hardly any other region in India is home to such great diversity. All these States are relatively small in size and smaller in population. None of them sends more than two members to the 541-seat parliament, contrasting starkly with Uttar Pradesh's 85 or Bihar's 54.

The North-East is constantly under the spotlight, drawing the attention of sociologists and federal administrators alike.

In ethnic terms, the 'Seven Sisters' constitute the Mongoloid fringe of India's North-East. Tribal culture dominates over large tracts. Early contacts with the rest of India brought Manipur and Tripura under Hindu influence and these became princely States under the British. Meghalaya, Nagaland and Mizoram are predominantly Christian, having been converted by European missionaries. Sikkim has a mixed Buddhist-Hindu population.

The 'Seven Sisters' are all mountainous, or have low hills, excepting international co-operation is now on the agenda. Nepal, Bhutan, Bangladesh and the north-eastern part of India are to be brought under a sub-regional plan for development within the framework of the seven-member South Asian Association for Regional Co-operation (SAARC).

Huge water resources and large mineral deposits make such development an attractive proposition. The 'Seven Sisters' need sensitive modernisation to enable them, while preserving their unique cultural and social values, to enjoy a higher standard of living.

Even in relative isolation, the region's culture has flourished. Manipur has, over the centuries, developed the classical dance form, *Manipuri*, which is on a par with *Bharat Natyam, Odissi Kuchipudi, Kathakali* and *Kathak*. Tribal art and culture have also been encouraged and supported by the government. Naga and Mizo dancers perform in New Delhi, and the region's skilled handicrafts can be bought in specialist shops.

Despite isolation, the region has not escaped outside influences with the result that new social relations have emerged. Tripura, Arunachal Pradesh and Sikkim have fared for the better. Tripura was entirely tribal, ruled by a Rajput king. But with Partition, millions of Hindu refugees fled East Pakistan, changing the State's demographic character. The process of assimilation, still incomplete, has sometimes aroused violent passions.

The people of Arunachal Pradesh, for long masters of their territory, have refused to accommodate the Chakma tribal refugees who fled

MEGHALAYA

In Sanskrit, Meghalaya is 'Abode of Clouds'. This former autonomous State within the State of Assam was created in 1969. Areas of the Cherrapunjee and Mawsynram are the wettest places in the world.

Population*	1.8 million
Area	22, 429 sq. km.
Population Density (per sq. km.)*	79
Population Growth (1981-1991)	32.9%
Principal Languages	Garo, Jaintia, Khasi and English
Capital	Shillong
Date of Statehood	January 21, 1972
Seats in Parliament - *Rajya Sabha: Lok Sabha*	1:2

* based on the 1991 Census

Agriculture:
83% of the population earn a living from the land. 27% of the cultivated land is under irrigation. Potato, tezpata, sugarcane, oilseeds, jute, cotton, mesta and arecanut are the main crops. Some areas grow high-yield paddy, wheat and maize, while vegetables and fruit are grown in the Khasi and Jaintia Hills. Famous for its oranges, pineapples, bananas, guavas, jackfruit, plums and pears.

Industry:
Forest and wood products provide a modest number of jobs. Deposits of coal, limestone, dolomite, felspar, quartz, glass sand and fire clay. Meghalaya produces 95% of the country's sillimanite. Cement is also produced.

NAGALAND

Formerly the Naga Hill district of Assam and the Tuensang Frontier of the North-East Frontier Agency (NEFA).

Population*	1.2 million
Area	16, 572 sq. km.
Population Density (per sq. km.)*	73
Population Growth (1981-1991)	56.1%
Principal languages	Angami, Ao, Chakhesang, Chang, Konyak, Lotha, Santam and Sema
Capital	Kohima
Date of Statehood	December 1, 1963
Seats in Parliament	
- *Rajya Sabha: Lok Sabha*	1:1

* based on 1991 Census

Agriculture:
Rice is the major crop cultivated by 90% of the inhabitants. Forest covers 17.5% of the area.

Industry:
Predominantly handloom enterprises. Deposits of coal, clay, glass, sand and limestone.

LEFT: *Ruins of the Kachari kingdom are a familiar sight in Nagaland. The Kachari, one of the Naga tribes, had established a Hindu kingdom before being displaced by the invading Buddhist Ahoms of Assam towards the end of the 17th century.*

SIKKIM

Formerly Gyalpo, this Himalayan Buddhist kingdom was founded in the 17th century. A referendum voted for full statehood within India. It shares its west border with Nepal, China is to the north and Bhutan is in the east.

Population*	406,000
Area	7, 096 sq. km.
Population Density (per sq. km.)*	57
Population Growth (1981-1991)	28.5%
Principal Languages	Bhutia, Lepcha, Limbu and Nepali
Capital	Gangtok
Date of Statehood	April 26, 1975
Seats in Parliament	
- Rajya Sabha: Lok Sabha	1:1

* based on 1991 Census

Agriculture:

A modest 12% of the land produces rice, maize, wheat, millet and barley. Alpine flowers, orchids and rhododendron are grown in the higher valleys and passes. Sikkim is the world's largest supplier of cardamom, a major cash crop. High quality apples and citrus fruit, such as orange and lemons, and pineapple are much in demand. A third of the State is forested.

Industry:

High-grade deposits of gold, silver, copper and zinc have recently been located. Handicrafts, such as wool and carpet weaving, are the more important and traditional industries. There is also some timber and wood products along with fruit preservation, watches and matches.

TRIPURA

Formerly a princely State of mostly tribal peoples which became a Union Territory. It is surrounded almost entirely by Bangladesh.

Population*	2.8 million
Area	10, 491 sq. km.
Population Density (per sq. km.)*	428
Population Growth (1981-1991)	34.3%
Principal Languages	Bengali, Kakborak and Manipuri
Capital	Agartala
Date of Statehood	January 21, 1972
Seats in Parliament - *Rajya Sabha : Lok Sabha*	1:2

* based on 1991 Census

Agriculture:
25% of the land area is cultivated with rice, jute, potato, oilseeds, mesta, sugarcane and cotton. 55% of the land is forested.

Industry:
Tea is the principal product from 56 tea gardens. Handloom weaving is the single largest industry. Aluminium utensils, steel furniture, pharmaceuticals, leather goods, fruit canning, oil and rice milling are also expanding.

lively festival. The English word juggernaut is derived from the temple's name. Then there is the *Bali Yatra* held at Cuttack in October, where for five consecutive days before the full moon, people sail colourful boats in memory of their ancestors who went to faraway lands to trade.

Orissa's forests cover more than a third of the State. There are many wildlife sanctuaries in these dense forests. Simlipal National Park is famous not only for its fauna but its tropical forests. Chikha is India's largest salt water lake and is separated from the Bay of Bengal by a sand bar and is the watering home for a large number of migratory birds.

PREVIOUS PAGE: **THE SUN TEMPLE** *in Konark dates back to the 13th century and was probably built by Orissan King Narashimhadev I. The temple is rich in elaborate carvings, sculptures and erotic figurines, similar to those at Khajuraho. It probably originated from a design for a chariot for the sun god, Surya. Around its base are twenty-four giant stone wheels. There are also seven gigantic stone horses pulling the 'chariot'.*

ORISSA

A former province of 25 separately ruled States merged with the Mayurbhanj State in 1949.

Population*	31.7 million
Area	155, 707 sq. km.
Population Density (per sq. km.)*	202
Population Growth (1981-1991)	20%
Principal Language	Oriya
Capital	Bhubaneswar
Major Port	Paradeep
Date of Statehood	August 19, 1949
Seats in Parliament - *Rajya Sabha : Lok Sabha*	10:21

* based on 1991 Census

Agriculture:

80% of the population produces 50% of the total output of the State. Rice is the principal crop, followed by pulses, oilseeds, jute, mesta, sugarcane, turmeric and coconut. Forests cover 43% of the land.

Industry:

Mineral reserves include manganese ore, limestone, dolomite, chromite, bauxite, graphite, china clay and nickel. Orissa is a leading producer of iron ore and most industries are mineral-based, including steel and a variety of ferro-alloys, such as pig iron, ferrochrome, aluminum. There is large scale cement and bamboo production.

ABOVE: *A quarter of Orissa's population are indigenous tribal peoples, or 'tribals'. There are more than 60 distinct groups and they tend to be concentrated in the hill areas along the coastal plain. The majority are Khondh, Santal, Soara, Juang, Parajas, Godabas and Koyas. Locals refer to the Bonda, another tribal group, as the 'naked people'.*

ABOVE: *Agricultural cultivation is the basis of Orissa's economy*

Punjab

THE NAME Punjab derives from the Farsi *Panj* (five) *Aab* (rivers), the land of five rivers: Jhelum, Chenab, Ravi, Beas and the Sutlej.

In 1947, when Pakistan was created out of India, Punjab was divided into two: the western half, with a predominantly Muslim population, went to Pakistan; the slightly smaller eastern half, where Hindus and Sikhs were in the majority, came to India. Both Pakistan and India retained the name Punjab, because on both sides of the dividing line the people spoke the same language and described themselves as Punjabis.

Indian Punjab was further divided in 1961 and the predominantly Hindi speaking areas of Haryana and Himachal Pradesh separated from it.

Punjab and Haryana share the same capital, Chandigarh, built near the Shivalik foothills in the 1950s.

Today's Indian Punjab, comprising of 50,362 square kilometres with 12 districts, has a population of a little over 20 million. Over 60 per cent of the population of Indian Punjab are Sikhs; a little over 35 per cent Hindus; the remainder are Christian or Muslims. Sikhs are largely peasant farmers living in villages. Hindus are tradesmen living in large towns and cities.

The Punjab landscape is flat; it has no hills or large lakes. It is hot and dusty during the summer months, but cold and fragrant in the winter. It is home to numerous places of pilgrimage for Sikhs, Hindus and Muslims alike. Amritsar - with its famous Golden Temple, the seat of the Sikh religion; Durgiana Temple (Hindu); and the Jallianwala Bagh where on 13 April 1919 (*Vaisakhi* - Punjab's New Year) General Dyer ordered troops to open fire on an unarmed congregation and killed over 370 men and women. People from all over the country come here to pay homage to the martyrs. At Sirhind is the mausoleum of a Muslim saint which attracts pilgrims from all over the sub-continent on his *urs* (death anniversary). There are innumerable forts, of which the ones in Phillour and Bahadurgarth (Patiala) are worth visiting.

Punjab is the most prosperous State of India. The per capita income of an average Punjabi is almost double that of the people of most Indian States and three times higher than that of Bihar. Its prosperity is largely based on agriculture. This is mostly due to the Green Revolution of the 1960s.

The most attractive part of the Punjab is its people. They are outgoing, uninhibited and extremely hospitable. The best time to see them enjoying themseves is on *Vaisakhi*, which is celebrated as harvest day with songs and dance. It is from here that the lively Bhangra dance found its way to the Diaspora.

RIGHT: *A Sikh funeral*

PUNJAB

From the Farsi words 'Panj' and 'Aab' - five rivers. The spiritual home for Sikhs.

Population*	20.3 million
Area	50, 362 sq. km.
Population Density (per sq. km.)*	403
Population Growth (1981-1991)	20.8%
Principal Language	Punjabi
Capital	Chandigarh
Date of Statehood	November 1, 1966
Seats in Parliament	
- *Rajya Sabha : Lok Sabha*	7:13

* based on 1991 Census

Agriculture:
84% of the total land area produces wheat and rice, plus maize, bajra, gram, barley and pulses. 75% of the population works on the land. Cash crops include cotton, oilseeds, sugarcane, tobacco and potato. The Punjab is the home of the 'Green Revolution' created by scientists from all over India.

Industry:
Small-scale manufacturing, primarily bicycles, bicycle and automobile parts, sewing machines, machine tools and parts, footwear and sports goods, surgical and scientific instruments. 70% of India's woollen hosiery is produced in the Punjab. Tractors, batteries, polyester fibres and nylon for hosiery are also responsible for the Punjab being the most prosperous State in India.

Rajasthan

RAJASTHAN, India's desert State, lies to the west of the country. The most striking feature is the Aravalli ranges, the oldest mountains in the world, dividing the State into two unequal halves. Three-fifths of the State to the northwest of the mountains contains the Great Indian Thar Desert, mostly sand and arid land. The southeastern part is higher and more fertile, with granite rocks and areas rich in silver, zinc and lead deposits.

Many parts of Rajasthan are older than the Himalayas, and it is therefore assumed that civilisation came to Rajasthan long before the rest of India. Numerous prehistoric and protohistoric sites exist to support this theory.

The Rajputana of old was inhabited by different ruling tribes till the foreign invasions of the second century before Christ. The Aryans, Greeks, Turks, Afghans, Persians and Mongols migrated to this region and produced a fascinating melting pot of some 200 ethnic groups. A mixture of these races, who survived all the upheavals of history, became the precursors of the Rajputs, the warrior class that ruled their fortified kingdoms. After the independence of India in 1947 this land was called Rajasthan, 'the abode of kings'.

Rajasthan is neither barren nor uninhabited. If anything, natural conditions have driven the people to live their lives with brilliant colours. The harsh dry climate has, however, forced them to evolve a semi-nomadic lifestyle. There are 20 royal houses of varying stature and the people still pay obeisance to them.

Rajasthan is predominantly an agricultural and pastoral State. The main language of the State is Rajasthani. Hinduism is the dominant religion, although Jainism is also important, and there are Muslim, Sikh and Christian minorities living in harmony.

The highly creative Rajasthanis have crafted works of style in stone, clay, leather, wood, ivory, glass and textiles. The kings and nobles were great patrons of the arts and encouraged artisans to set up schools for their crafts, and to this day one can find people practicing crafts handed down by their ancestors.

LEFT: **HAWA MAHAL** - *Palace of the Winds - is part of the east wall of Jaipur ('the pink city') a classic example of Rajput architecture and artistry, and a very recognisable landmark. The five-storey, sandstone palace was built in 1799 by Maharajah Sawai Pratap Singh. Semi-octagonal, honeycombed windows allowed the women of the royal household to discreetly watch the processions on the city's main street. A series of brass wind vanes on multi-levels were dextrously positioned and set in assorted directions to indicate wind direction. Jaipur, the capital of Rajasthan, was painted pink for the visit of Prince Albert in 1853.*

RAJASTHAN

'Land of Kings', a union of princely States, formerly the United States of Greater Rajasthan in 1949. Shares northern border with Pakistan.

Population*	44 million
Area	342, 239 sq. km.
Population Density (per sq. km.)*	129
Population Growth (1981-1991)	28.4%
Principal Languages	Rajasthani and Hindi
Capital	Jaipur
Date of Statehood	November 1, 1956
Seats in Parliament	
- Rajya Sabha: Lok Sabha	10:25

* based on 1991 Census

Agriculture:
Only 19% of the total cultivated land is irrigated and jowar, bajra, wheat, maize, barley and gram, oilseeds, sugarcane, cotton and tobacco are the major crops.

Industry:
The State provides all of India's lead and zinc concentrates, emeralds and garnets, 94% of its gypsum, 84% of its asbestos, 76% of its silver ore, 68% of felspar and 12% of the country's mica. There are also rich salt deposits and Khetri and Dariba are copper mining centres. Industries include textiles, rugs and woollen goods, sugar, cement, glass, sodium, oxygen and acetylene, pesticides, insecticides and dyes. Rajasthan is celebrated for its imaginative handicrafts, marble works, carpets, leather, pottery, jewellery and embroidery.

The people of Rajasthan have a passion for dancing, singing, drama, devotional music, puppet shows and other festivities. Each region has its own folk entertainment. Not only do the dance styles and songs differ, even the musical instruments are varied.

The better known festivals are the Nagaur Cattle Fair and the Desert Festival in Jaisalmer in February. The Elephant Festival in Jaipur during March, the Marwar Festival in Jodhpur in October, the Pushkar Fair near Ajmer in November and the Camel Festival at Bikaner in January are hugely popular.

While the princes built the stately palaces and forts, their nobles were not far behind in building impressive *havelis*. Most of the palaces are still used by the erstwhile royal families, though some have had sections converted into museums and hotels. The conversion of havelis into Heritage Hotels is catching on. They offer more than five-star treatment and are extremely popular with visitors.

ABOVE: *Camel safaris are frequent in the arid Thar desert*

OPPOSITE: *Rajasthani fairs are a riot of colour and dancing*

Tamil Nadu

TAMIL NADU is a State where the present exists in a continuous process of recreation through reference to the past. It set a trend for the whole country to emulate when it changed its name from the British-derived 'Madras', to the authentically national 'Tamil Nadu'. The renaming of the capital city followed.

The multitude of temples that cover the Tamil Nadu landscape, with their magnificent architecture, provide a living retrospect of the region's successive political dynasties. Temples continue to be the focus of much social life in Tamil Nadu.

Tamil Nadu politics has been dominated for over three decades by an explicitly rational, not to say, atheistic strain. The debunking of the claims of spiritual gurus and the hereditary priesthood was a vital part of the evolution of the modern Tamil consciousness. It was aimed at the elimination of the privileged Brahminic caste hierarchy, and this was the prelude to a revolution that gave birth to a merit-based society. Tamil Nadu has struck many a blow for reason and enlightenment and is a pioneer charting a course for the rest of the country to follow.

Unlike other popular film genres, Tamil cinema has largely steered clear of mythological themes. The heroes and icons of Tamil cinema are either fictional creations or historical figures elevated to the status of demi-god. Cinema and theatre personalities were prominent in the early movements of Tamil cultural resistance, whether against colonialism or domination from the north. Popular fantasies finally crystallised into real life in 1977, when a film star best known for his heroic portrayals on screen became chief minister of the State.

Tamil Nadu's contributions to the realm of science have been noteworthy. Two of the three Indian-born Nobel Laureates in the sciences hailed from Tamil Nadu.

ABOVE: **UDHAGAMANDALAM**
*(Ootacamund or Ooty) hill
station, popular with the British,
is famed for its walks along leafy,
winding lanes. Ooty is a favoured
destination, not only for
foreigners, but also for the locals.
It boasts a famous public school.*

RIGHT: **THE SHORE TEMPLE**
*in Mahaballipuram, buffeted by
wind and sea, is a fine example of
the late Pallava period. Built in
the 7th century, it is a World
Heritage building.*

TAMIL NADU

*The core of Dravidian culture, formerly Madras. The State dates back 6,000 years. The
Mughal invasions had less impact on the Dravadian culture than the arrival of the East
India Company in Madras in 1639.*

Population *	55.7 million
Area	130, 058 sq. km.
Population Density (per sq. km.) *	429
Population Growth (1981-1991)	15.4%
Principal Language	Tamil
Capital	Chennai (formerly Madras)
Major ports	Chennai, Tuticorin
Date of Statehood	November 1, 1956
Seats in Parliament - *Rajya Sabha: Lok Sabha*	18:39

* based on 1991 Census

Agriculture:
70% of the population is involved, while 48% of the cultivated land is under irrigation.
Commercial crops include groundnut, cotton, chilli, sugarcane, ginger, coconut,
tobacco, coffee, tea, and rubber. Principal food crops are rice, milletts, ragi, pulses,
bajra, jowar, onions, potato and sweet potato. 17% of the land is forested.

Industry:
Mineral reserves include limestone, magnesite, mica, quartz felspar, salt, bauxite,
lignite, gypsum and fireclay. Major manufacturing involves cotton textiles, silk,
leather tanning, cement, chemicals, fertiliser, paper and associated products. Heavy
engineering includes diesel engines, automobiles and bicycles, railway wagons and
coaches. The State is an important exporter of tanned skins, hides and leather goods,
cotton piece goods, tea, coffee, spices and tobacco. Chennai is a major centre of the
film industry.

PREVIOUS PAGE: **MEENAKSHI - SUNDARESHWARAR TEMPLE** *is in Madurai, capital of the Pandya kings of 2,000 years ago. It is part of a temple complex, which has twelve towers. These gopura reach up to 50 metres in height and are covered with hundreds of thousands of brightly coloured statues, which represent gods and demons. Madurai is derived from the Tamil word madhuram, which means sweetness. Shiva is said to have shook his hair over the city, sprinkling it with amrita, the nectar of immortality.*

Uttar Pradesh

IN THE far north, the snow covered Himalayan mountains loom large. Nestling in the lower ranges are picturesque hills and valleys with snow-fed fast-flowing rivers heading for the fertile Gangetic plain. These stretch south of the Himalayas and spread out into the northern parts of the central Indian plateau. The Ganges and its many tributaries are among the many rivers that have made Uttar Pradesh so fertile.

Because of its sensitive position in the heart of the Indo-Gangetic plain, Uttar Pradesh was the victim of many incursions, throughout which she was never a passive spectator, its people bravely defending its borders, sometimes successfully, and occasionally suffering temporary set backs, but for the most part assimilating the invader without compromising territorial integrity. Much of Vedic literature originated here, as did the great Indian epics, the *Ramayana* and the *Mahabharata*. The Buddhist-Hindu period in Uttar Pradesh, with its brilliant sculptors and architects, added glory and lustre to the artistically priceless Indian heritage.

Paintings, music and dance were a most enjoyable pursuit. It was truly an affirmation of art for art's sake.

Hindi and Urdu continued to flourish in harmony under the Mughals. Much of the musical tradition in Uttar Pradesh was developed during this period. This gave birth to the sitar, a stringed instrument of the lute family, and the tabla, two small drums, the most popular instruments of north Indian music. The spirited *kathak* classical dance style is still the most popular in northern India.

Bhadohi and Mirzapur are famous for carpet weaving, and Lucknow for its *chikan* embroidery. Moradabad is noted for metal enamelling, Varanasi for brocades and silk, and Nagina for ebony work. New techniques and styles in the age-old craft of glass products manufacture has put Ferozabad on the international map.

West Bengal

WEST BENGAL is the truncated third of the province of Bengal in British India, the rest of which was transferred to Pakistan 50 years ago and is now the independent state of Bangladesh. Traditionally in the vanguard of social and political movements, this eastern State has overcome the trauma of Partition and its exodus of millions of uprooted humans.

The original seat of the imperial power, it suffered economic exploitation, but also benefited from western education and science. The Bengali personified the enlightened Indian, and was rebellious.

Rebellion was not a transitory phase and economic decline sharpened as private capital moved to other parts of India. Rootless refugees began to swarm the urban settlements. An exasperated Nehru called Calcutta "a city of processions, of nightmares". His despairing grandson, Rajiv Gandhi said the Bengali capital was a "dying city".

But West Bengal refused to die. In the first decades of independence, while it languished industrially, it achieved remarkable progress in rural reforms, social development and agriculture. Now, the State is poised once again for an industrial take-off.

West Bengal produced the cinematic genius, Satyajit Ray. He led and inspired a school of film-makers, some of the best in the world. Calcutta annually stages India's most popular book fair, where men and women queue for hours to gain entry.

West Bengal, known for its disdain for orthodox politics, has been ruled by Marxists for two decades. It is also a tolerant and rational State, a safe haven for religious minorities, some of whom can feel uncomfortable in certain parts of India. Calcutta prides itself on its association with Mother Teresa.

West Bengal seems to be moving towards a new dawn. It is now able to feed its 60 million people; it has overcome a chronic energy shortage, and its Marxist government, in the style of Deng Xiaoping's 'socialism with Chinese characteristics', is embracing the free-market.

There is also a blitz to clean up Calcutta, remove the garbage from the

WEST BENGAL

Under British rule it was made part of a province also comprising Orissa, Bihar and Assam in 1863. By 1905 this area was divided into East and West Bengal; the former became Bangladesh after the war of independence in 1971. Nepal and Bhutan share its northern border in the north.

Population*	68.1 million
Area	88, 752 sq. km.
Population Density (per sq. km.)*	767
Population Growth (1981-1991)	24.7%
Principal Language	Bengali
Capital	Calcutta
Date of Statehood	November 1, 1956
Seats in Parliament	
- *Rajya Sabha: Lok Sabha*	16:42

* based on 1991 Census

Agriculture:

55% of the population produces 50% of the State's income. 45% of the total cultivated area is under irrigation. The State's mainstay is jute (nearly 60% of the nation's total output) and it is the second largest tea producer (nearly 25%) and the third largest producer of rice, whose cultivation accounts for 88% of the total cropped area. Gram, barley, betel leaf, linseed, mustard and rape, sugarcane, maize, cotton and tobacco are other important crops. 13% of the State is forested.

Industry:

The three principal minerals are coal, china clay and dolomite. There are also deposits of limestone, copper, iron, silica, quartz, rock phosphate, manganese and sandstone. West Bengal is the leading industrial State, with more than 20% of all registered factories. Economic activity includes two steel plants and aluminum, electronics, automobiles and bicycles, chemicals and pharmaceuticals, leather goods and footwear, jute, tea, cotton, textiles and silk, paper, glass, timber processing, dairy products, paper and fertiliser.

PREVIOUS PAGE: **HOOGHLY RIVER** *at Diamond Harbour. This resort, a little over 50 kilometres from Calcutta, is close to the mouth of the Ganga in the Bay of Bengal.*

OPPOSITE: **DARJEELING** *has seventy-eight tea gardens which produce nearly 25 per cent of India's tea. Almost 50,000 people are involved in picking, pressing, fermenting and sorting the tea - regarded as the world's best in terms of quality. There is an increasing use of modern technology with innovations including clonal replanting.*

BELOW: **TERRACOTTA TEMPLES** *at Bishnipur, with finely carved depictions of scenes from the Ramayana*

streets and clear the pavements of squatters. The city is the only one in India to boast an underground rail network.

The imposing National Museum, the National Library and the Asiatic Society buildings could do with an urgent face-lift. It should also be noted that West Bengal is the only State in the country with both sea-shore and snow-capped mountains.

Everybody knows old Calcutta, as static as the Howrah Bridge. But the old yields to the new, and the modern and cheerful Vidyasagar Setu (bridge) symbolises the renewal that will make of West Bengal a land for all its people.

ABOVE: *Brightly painted fishing boats line the harbour in Diu*

PREVIOUS PAGE: *An Andamanese girl*

Across the Seven Seas:
The Indian Diaspora

THE Indian Diaspora dates back some two millennia, when traders, scholars and settlers followed in the wake of the Indian colonisers of a number of Asian countries. Traders and merchants also settled in parts of the Middle East.

However, it is the relatively recent settlements over the last two centuries that mainly concern us in this essay.

The Indian Diaspora extends to most parts of the world - North, West, East and South Africa; Malaya, long before it evolved into Malaysia and Singapore; Fiji; the Caribbean; Japan, where the Indian settlement, unknown to many, is over a hundred years old; and, latterly, the economic migration to Europe, North America and Australasia.

From the 1840s, waves of migrants left India for the British owned and run sugar and rubber plantations of South Africa, Fiji, Malaya, Mauritius and the Caribbean. This migration was forced on the Indian people by the poverty and joblessness of Empire. It was a cruel and heartless affair, a terrible saga of exploitation and degradation in conditions little removed from chattel slavery itself. Hundreds of thousands of families were uprooted and transported across rough seas in barely seaworthy boats to culturally alien conditions in a racist and near-lawless environment, where they became simply beasts of prey, whose sole purpose was to produce the maximum profit for their greedy masters. Thousands of men and women died at sea, stricken by disease and the lack of proper medical care, or simply of broken hearts and dreams.

Likewise, countless Sikh labourers were to suffer and perish while building the Canadian Pacific Railways across such harsh and inhospitable terrain as the Rocky Mountains.

An English politician, Lord John Russell, described the conditions of Indian indentured labourers as a "new system of slavery." He was not wrong. Such was the protection given to kith and kin exploiters by the British rulers, that those brave Indians who dared to expose the cruelty of the planters were harshly punished. When the courageous Indian doctor, John Henry Ponampalam, spoke out against the appalling mistreatment of south Indian labourers forced into slavery on the rubber plantations of Malaya, the British rulers arrested him on trumped-up charges and imposed a huge fine, which nearly bankrupted the altruistic doctor.

In South Africa, Mahatma Gandhi had to deal with innumerable cases of beatings of men and women workers, and of thieving planters, who not only frequently cheated their employees of their wages, but compelled them to spend whatever little money they managed to obtain, on the ridiculously over-priced products from the planters' stores.

It was the same throughout the Caribbean, as well as in Fiji and Mauritius. Their terrible ordeal has been recorded by many sympathetic white and Indian historians. India, to its credit, even though not then a free nation, protested against these abuses and demanded an end to indentured labour.

The British government responded with empty rhetoric, deploring the behaviour of their brutal brethren in Natal, Trinidad, British Guiana, Malaya, Mauritius and Fiji, while at the same time refusing to actually act against the white plantocracy. Gandhi even went to England from South Africa to personally plead with the British government for an improvement in living conditions. But little was done until the Indian colonial legislature unilaterally decided to ban the export of Indian labour to the British colonies. Things then improved, but only slightly.

The indentured labourers were invariably followed by traders and merchants, eager to cater for the special cultural needs of the labourers and also to trade with the more privileged whites.

The Indian diaspora in South Africa were responsible for the first *Satyaghra*, or non-violent campaign, in history. Masterminded by Gandhi, this struggle did not achieve all its aims, for the Indians were to remain a disenfranchised and oppressed people until the destruction of apartheid. However, the Resistance did achieve some notable victories, especially the abolition of the hated poll tax on Indians of all classes. It was undoubtedly this success, on a small, but significant scale, that persuaded Gandhi to experiment with *Satyaghra* on a larger canvass in his own beloved India.

The South African *Satyaghra* campaign succeeded not only because of the wise leadership of Gandhi, but equally because of the discipline and courage of the indentured labourers. In the summer of 1997, a long-overdue memorial to one of the great heroines of the struggle, 16-year-old Valliamma R. Munuswami, was unveiled in Johannesburg. Valliamma, a bright, brave and attractive young woman, with a surprisingly mature political consciousness, had crossed the border into the Transvaal in defiance of a preposterous law which restricted the Indians to Natal, denying them the right of settlement in the other provinces.

Valliamma was arrested and thrown into prison. She entered it a tall and healthy girl but the brutal regime took its toll. When she left jail, thin, emaciated and barely able to speak, she had lost none of the proud defiance which had cast such a magnetic spell on the community of resisters. She should have been at school, enjoying a care-free existence like any other 16-year-old. But the times were wickedly out of joint. Valliamma R. Munuswami's dignified bearing and stubborn determination to fight injustice to the bitter end symbolises not just the magnificent resistance of indentured labourers in South Africa but throughout the far-flung British Empire.

The later South African struggle against apartheid also produced many outstanding freedom fighters. The newspapers of the day bristle with names like Pillay, Naidoo and Moodley, men and women who frequently violated racist laws without fear for the consequences. Many press clippings are framed on the walls of *Anand Bhavan*, former residence of the Nehru family, and now a museum.

The most revered of Gandhi's lieutenants was Thumbi Naidoo. The Naidoos are probably the most remarkable Indian political family in South Africa, with an unbroken tradition of active involvement in the anti-racist movement, from Gandhi's *Satyaghra* campaign through to the destruction of apartheid. The illustrious Thumbi Naidoo passed the baton on to his son, Roy Naran Naidoo, who also died with his boots on, a bloodied but unbowed warrior against the Smuts and Malan regimes. Roy was a close associate, and intimate friend of Nelson Mandela, Walter Sisulu

and Oliver Tambo, regular visitors to the Naidoo home in Johannesburg. It is not disrespectful to say of this obdurate man, who lived for the revolution, that he was a fanatic. He brought up his family, three sons and two daughters, to be loyal and active members of the Resistance, even if this meant they had to suffer torture, prison and death. Nothing, he told them, not even their personal happiness or well-being, must take precedence over the anti-apartheid war. His family, including his equally courageous wife, Manonmoney, lived up to this valiant tradition. Four generations are heroically represented among the 'jail birds' and the victims of apartheid torture.

The best known of the third generation of the Naidoo family was Shanthi, a delicate girl with the courage of a lioness. Shanthi was at Winnie Mandela's side in a highly secretive operation against the regime. The South African police had picked up Winnie, but had no case against her. The police needed one of her closest associates to spill the beans. Shanthi was arrested in a midnight swoop, became one of the many "disappeared," with her family being deliberately kept in the dark, not knowing whether she was alive or dead. Shanthi was driven to a remote prison, condemned to solitary confinement and tortured, but this proud granddaughter of the equally proud Thumbi Naidoo, refused to betray Winnie, with the result that a very serious case, which would have resulted in a long prison sentence, was dropped.

There were other freedom fighting titans among South Africa's Indians, the best known and best loved of them being Dr. Yusuf Mohammed Dadoo, Dr. Mohambury Naicker, Ahmed Kathrada, Billy Nair, H.A.Naidoo and M.D. Naidoo. The Indian people of South Africa, at under a million, are a fraction of the overall population, but thanks to men and women of this calibre, and thousands of others, many of whom were jailed, tortured or killed, they were strongly and honourably represented in the fight against apartheid. Indeed, in the early 1990s, a South African Indian doctor, Moosajee Bhamjee, was even elected to the Irish Dail (Parliament), representing that country's Labour Party. His rural constituency had never elected a Labour member before.

This is equally the story of Indians everywhere in the diaspora, invariably identifying themselves with the struggles of their nations for freedom and justice.

However, history and circumstances singled out Guyana to produce the diaspora's greatest son. Dr. Cheddi Jagan, the President of Guyana, who died in 1997, was a statesman of world stature, a socialist, anti-racist and anti-colonial warrior of the noblest kind.

In the mould of one of Dr. Jagan's compatriot's, Sir Shridath Ramphal, a former Guyanese foreign minister who became Commonwealth Secretary-General and held the post for 15 years, played a vital role in the international campaign to isolate apartheid South Africa, and hasten the advent of a non-racial democracy. Like Nehru and Cheddi Jagan, Ramphal also subscribed to the view that politics required a moral dimension.

Ramphal rarely engaged in rhetoric. Substance was his forte. He worked feverishly behind the scenes to destroy the untenable thesis that white South Africa should be "persuaded" to mend its ways! Ramphal astutely created a powerful coalition of disparate forces against apartheid, including India, Australia, New Zealand and Canada, and, significantly, Britain's Queen Elizabeth II. When it came to the question of apartheid, Queen Elizabeth appeared to turn for advice to the Commonwealth Secretary-General, for whom she had a high and affectionate regard.

On his first visit to Britain after his release, in 1991, Nelson Mandela paid a warm, heartfelt tribute to Sir Shridath Ramphal for his role both in securing his own release and in winning the freedom of his people.

Among other principled politicians of Indian descent who have risen to the highest office are Basdeo Panday, a trade union leader of the sugarcane workers who became Prime Minister of Trinidad and Tobago, and Sir Seewoosagur Ramgoolam, who led Mauritius to independence, becoming that country's first Prime Minister, a position held at time of writing by his son, Navin Ramgoolam.

The Indian diaspora in Britain may have been small in the late 19th and early 20th centuries, but it was by no means devoid of drama or achievement. Britain's first Indian MP was Dadabhai Naoroji, businessman, intellectual and patriot extraordinary who earned for himself the sobriquet, the Father of the Indian Nation. Others who followed in his wake were Sir Mancherjee Bhownagree and Shapurji Saklatvala. Saklatvala was a member of the famous Tata family but he made no secret of his contempt for capitalism. He championed not simply the cause of Indian liberation, but also dramatically highlighted the iniquity of an Empire, which though indecently rich at Indian, Chinese and African expense, was plagued in its own homeland by widescale social and economic injustice. Saklatvala fearlessly championed the British oppressed, even as he worked for the expulsion of the British Occupation of his native land.

The much larger Indian diaspora, which first arrived on Britain's shores in the late forties and the early fifties, has in a short space of time made a powerful impact on the nation's cultural, academic,

"I should be unwilling to adopt any measure to favour the transfer of labourers from British India to Guiana....I am not prepared to encounter the responsibility of a measure which may lead to a dreadful loss of life on one hand, or, on the other, to a new system of slavery."

Lord John Russell
15 February 1840

business and professional life. Perhaps it is in the culinary field that the Indian community's impact on British life has been most striking and most pervasive. Nowadays even the smallest village boasts an Indian restaurant, and fish and chips has long since been supplanted as Britain's national dish by curry, rice and dahl. The Labour election victory of May 1 1997 led to the appointment of the first member of a British government of Indian origin, when Keith Vaz, who had first been elected for the constituency of Leicester East in 1987, was appointed Parliamentary Private Secretary to the Attorney-General.

However, one last word needs to be said regarding the historic pioneers of the diaspora - regardless of how brutal or oppressive their circumstances were, the indentured labourers never gave way to despair. They may have longed in the early stages for a return to the beloved country - some actually did so - but the vast majority realised there was no turning back, that, for better or worse, they had become South Africans, Trinidadians, Fijians, Guyanese, Malaysians, Surinamese or Mauritians. That being the case, they got on with the job of building for their children a brighter future, in much the same way as the Indians of the British, European and North American diaspora are doing today, while at the same time retaining everything vital in their humane and tolerant culture, something that has not only enriched their own lives, but also benefited the various peoples among whom destiny has decreed that they coexist peacefully and productively.

OPPOSITE: **INDIA IN BRITAIN.**
Diana, Princess of Wales visits the Swaminarayan Hindu Temple in Neasden, north London, the largest Hindu temple in Europe.

Ramparts of Valour:

India's soldiers in Britain's wars

IN AN unusual departure from the then customary practice of downplaying the prowess and achievements of the Indian Army in World War II, General Wavell said of the Fourth Indian Division's triumph in the Italian Campaign: "The fame of this division will surely go down as one of the greatest fighting formations in military history."

This glorious chapter, one of many in the history of the Indian Army, has been relegated to obscure archives, whereas its real place is in blockbuster novels and Hollywood .

However, not a single Western film or novel has ever dramatised their incredible feats.

The Indian Army's prodigious achievements, which serious historians agree brought a just peace quicker in a war which had threatened to drag on for a few more years, has still not been given its proper due by the West. Winston Churchill, Britain's wartime leader, gave strict instructions to his propaganda division and the British media not to mention, let alone give prominence to the Indian annihilation of the 'Aryan' Germans, the self-proclaimed Japanese supermen and the less than enthusiastic Italians. Yet it remains a fact that the Indians won the highest number of VCs (Victoria Cross) for their exceptional exploits of valour on the battlefield.

Indian troops left their indelible footprints on the shores of Italy, Sicily, Africa, the Middle East, Malaya, Singapore and Burma, and not for the first time.

In the second half of the 19th century, too, many Indians had rallied to the defence and preservation of an Empire which also sat so heavily on their backs. Indian troops are still remembered for their famous expeditions to feudal China in 1860 and 1900. Indian contingents were also at the centre of the bitter fighting in the Abyssinian Campaign in 1868. The Indian armoured forces engaged in two fierce wars in Afghanistan in 1879 and 1880 to keep the paws of the Russian Bear away from the British Empire. Indian warriors were likewise active in Egypt in 1882 and in Burma in 1885.

Then there were the local wars in India's backyard, in Nepal, Nagaland and Lusai. As usual, when others were timidly taking cover behind them, the sons of India led from the front in Malta and Cyprus in 1884. Future historians of Empire, from the Indian side of course, will probably quite rightly infer from this indispensability of the Indian Army that the Empire might not have survived for as long as it did without

their valorous sacrifice and their tactical and strategic skills. This is what probably caused the British General, Sir Archibald Galloway, to hold them up as role models to white British soldiers: "You ought to join the Indian Army."

In the First World War, Indian troops saw action in France and Belgium, Gallipoli, Salonika and Palestine, Egypt and Sudan, Mesopotamia, the Cameroons and East Africa, Somaliland, Aden, and in the region around the Red Sea, Persia, Kurdistan and remote North China. They did not flinch in the face of vicious poison gas attacks by the Germans at Ypres, were unruffled by the slush and mush of the Somme or the fearsome tanks of the enemy at Cambrai. They were part of Allenby's legendary force which captured 75,000 German and Turkish prisoners in Palestine. Battle honours belonged to them in Gallipoli, Aden and Kiliminjaro. Theirs was a continuous and seemingly unending attachment to the battlefield, their skills and bravery unmatched.

By 1918, India had sent 1,302,394 troops to fight in what some Indian and Third World historians describe as the Great European War. 138,000 troops fought in France, 675,000 in Mesopotamia, and 144,000 in Egypt. Together these constituted the three main theatres of the war.

The Navy and the Air Force also grew correspondingly. The Royal Flying Corps (RFC) provided air cover for the army which had a number of outstanding Indian officers, two of whom fell together with their men in the early battles. These two officers were posthumously awarded the DFC (Distinguished Flying Cross.)

The RFC developed into a powerful arm of the ground forces during World War II. Two million Indian troops, with 5,000 officers, participated in this conflict.

The much feared Indian divisions, who struck terror into an enemy over whom they had the psychological edge on account of the reputation that preceded them, spread out over the world's war fronts. In one of the most arduous campaigns in military history, from Hannibal and Caesar downwards, the Eighth Indian Army marched from the gates of Cairo, along the African shores, across to Sicily, and ultimately on to the gates of Rome. The Panzer Corps fought with might and main, but they were no match for the Indians. It was primarily thanks to the Eighth Army that the Allies were able to put paid to the soft underbelly of Europe. The 4th, 5th, 8th and 210th

Indian Divisions mercilessly crushed the Germans and Italians at Sangria, Anzio, Cassino and Monastery Hill.

In Asia, which the well-oiled and highly efficient Japanese fighting machine threatened to over-run, the Indian Army was assigned the tricky task of preventing an allied rout. The Indians bore the brunt of the Japanese attacks, while other so-called seasoned soldiers were often nowhere to be seen. This gave rise to the joke that the "English will never be slaves, they will always fight to the last Indian, Irishman and Scot!"

The Indians suffered some terrible reverses but they stood firm and gradually turned the tide against the much vaunted 'invincible' Japanese war machine. But not before the Japanese took Hong Kong, overran Malaya, walked over Rangoon and inflicted the greatest humiliation ever in the Asian campaign - a numerically smaller number of Japanese contemptuously took Singapore, which Winston Churchill had described as "an impregnable fortress". The Japanese took 38,496 British troops, 67,340 Indian and 18,490 Australian prisoners.

The Japanese were now poised for their attack on India, which they hoped to invade with the help of the Indian National Army founded by Subhas Chandra Bose.

But they still had to reckon with the under-rated power of the Indian Army. It was here that the Indians - though at a serious disadvantage against the Japanese in terms of weapons, equipment and aircraft, with the British concentrating their major weapons, equipment and aircraft in the European theatre - spectacularly reversed the familiar syndrome of Japanese 'invincibility.' The harsh and hostile terrain of Burma and Assam, with unmapped mountains, jungles, treacherous rapids, swift- flowing rivers and a continuous six-month rain, failed to dampen the ardour of the Indians to get even with the Japanese. The deadly malaria took its toll of many soldiers but was never allowed to undermine morale. The Japanese were resolute and determined. But the 14th Indian Army covered itself in glory, effectively putting an end to the remorseless and relentless Japanese march of triumph.

Neither side gave any quarter. They were too proud and honourable to cut their losses and run, as was so poignantly illustrated on the Southern perimeter. 'O' Company, which had stood in the way of what could have been the decisive Japanese advance, was wiped out. There were no survivors. In the morning light the body of the section commander, Lance Naik Joigraj, was discovered. He was still clutching his rifle, with a bloodstained bayonet, while around him lay eight enemy soldiers, done to death by Naik Jograj's bayonet.

The Indian Army continued to carry the 'white man's burden' in Sicily and the Middle East and, even after the War, the British continued to deploy them in the Far East until 1946. The famous Indian Fourth Division only came back to India five years later.

As Nehru has reminded us, India not only gave its grandest manhood to the War, it also financed it to the tune of several billion pounds, all of which was collected through punitive taxes. The Indian economy also suffered, as consumer production was halted to give way to production for war, uniforms and materials.

Without the Indians, it is probable that the whole of Asia would have fallen to Japan and the flag of the Third Reich would have been flying over the British Parliament. But there was little gratitude and even less recognition for these fallen and surving heroes, save for some medals.

However, fortunately for the Indian people their capable and conscientious historians have redressed this unacceptable imbalance in a number of histories.

All the wars in which the Indians were on the very front-line, were European conflicts in which Indian soldiers defended the vital imperialist interests of the British nation, a fact which is too often overlooked.

Indian generosity, courage, decency and magnanimity are memorably evoked by one of India's most loved feminists and poets, Sarojini Naidu:

"Lo I have flung to the East and the West
priceless treasures torn form my breast,
and yielded the sons of my stricken womb
to the drum beats of England and sabres of doom
Gathered like pearls in their alien graves
silent they sleep in Persian waves;
scattered like shell in Egyptian sands
they lie with pale brows and brave broken hands.
They are strewn like blossoms mown down by chance
on the blood brown meadows of Flanders and France

Oh England! Oh world
Remember the blood of my slaughtered ones
weep for my dead, my martyed sons."

Lord Wavell, Viceroy of India, presents the Victoria Cross to Sepoy Bandari Ram of the 10th Baluch Regiment, for his heroic actions in a battle in East Mayu, Arakan, on 22 November 1944

1757 The first rupee coin of East India Company was minted in Calcutta.

1758 Separate courts were constituted for Indians and Europeans by the East India Company.

1760 After their victory against the French, the British had virtually no European opponent left in India.

1764 The European Bengal Regiment mutinied, followed by the first Indian Sepoy Mutiny, many mutineers were put to death.

1765 The takeover of 'Diwani' was a notable landmark in the political and constitutional history of British India, which was taken as the beginning of British rule. Clive, Governor of Bengal.

1766 Official postal system introduced.

1767 Survey of India (which discovered Mount Everest) was founded.

1769 The first organised horse-racing in India took place at Akra, near Calcutta.

1770 The first financial bank under European direction established in Calcutta. Over 3,000,000 dead as plague and famine rage through Bengal.

1771 Madras Race Course, first in country.

1772 Ram Mohan Roy was born on 22 May. He founded the Hindu College in 1817 and Brahmo Samaj in 1828, was a protagonist for the abolition of 'Suttee'. Muslim Personal Law, based on the Shariat, was first enacted by the British.

1774 Narayan Rao's son was installed as Peshwa Madhav Rao the Second, when only 10 days old. The first licence for digging and selling coal was issued by East India Company

1778 Grenadiers were formed for the first time in the Indian army. The first printed Bengali book was published.

1780 The first newspaper in India *Hicky's Bengal Gazette* was published in English in Calcutta. Maharaja Ranjit Singh was born on 13 November, he built a large empire and commanded India's most powerful fighting force in a thousand-years, controlling the entrance to the Khyber Pass.

1782 First home for the aged was started in Madras.

1784 The first newspaper of Madras, *The Madras Courier* was published. The Preventive Detention Act was introduced in India. Pitt's India Act passed in British parliament.

1787 The Indian Botanic Garden was founded near Calcutta.

1788 The *Calcutta Gazette* was first published. Port Blair got its name from Lt. Archibald Blair who surveyed the 258 Andaman and 56 Nicobar islands.

1789 The first weekly newpaper of Bombay, the *Bombay Herald* published.

1790 Export of fine 'Muslin' cloth of Bengal was banned by East India Company.

1792 First Indian cricket club started at Eden Gardens in Calcutta.

1793 Lord Cornwallis decided that Indians be excluded from India's administration service.

1795 15th Battalion Bengal Native Infantry refused to board the two ships bound for Malacca, they were quickly suppressed by heavy cannon fire and the battalion disbanded.

1797 Lord Cornwallis was sworn in as Governor General of India for the second time, however, he did not arrive in India until 1805.

1799 During the last Mysore war, Tipu Sultan was the only Indian king who died on the battlefield, fighting the British. He was cremated by the British with the full pomp and splendour due to a Sultan.

1800 The first English teaching school established in Calcutta.

1801 The Bombay Army went to fight in Egypt, (to Mauritius, 1810 and to Iran, 1856). The first printed Bengali book was published.

1802 The first century in cricket was scored on Indian soil in Calcutta.

1803 In the treaty of Surji Arjangaon, the British acquired control of Delhi, Agra, Broach and other territories. This was in fact the end of the Mughal Empire. Lord Wellesley suppressed the sacrificing of children in the sea in Sagar Island in fulfilment of vows.

1805 Lord Cornwallis died only eight weeks after his arrival in Ghazipur.

1806 Indian forces at Vellore and Madras mutinied because they were forbidden to wear caste-marks and earrings during parade, as a result 500 were slaughtered.

1809 Bank of Bengal, also known as Presidency Bank, was established.

1811 Importation of slaves into India was forbidden.

1813 The first boat races took place in Calcutta on the Hooghly river.

1814 Calcutta Museum established.

1815 The first iron smelter was established in Madras. The first iron bridge was built over Gomti river near Lucknow.

1816 Nepal withdrew from Sikkim.

1817 The Ajanta cave temples were discovered quite by accident. Gujarat came under British rule.

1818 India's first cotton mill was established in Calcutta.

1819 The first concerted effort for the spread of female education was made by Calcutta Female Juvenile Society. Calcutta Race Course was constructed.

1820 Ishwar Chandra Vidyasagar led the movement for widow remarriage and abolition of polygamy in Hindu society.

1821 Ram Mohan Roy founded the first nationalist press. The first lithographic printing of a picture was done in Calcutta. The first lighthouse was set up on Sagar Island.

1822 First Gujarati newspaper, the *Bombay Samachar*, published.

1823 The first steamship was built in Calcutta. The first coffee plantation was opened. Sanskrit College started in Calcutta to teach traditional studies.

1824 Edward Page gave orders to fire on 47th Native Infantry who revolted against being sent to Burma, sixty were gunned down and two dozen were executed. The Calcutta merchants voted a lakh of rupees for the first person who would navigate a steamship to India. Dutch land possessions in India were taken over by the British in exchange for Sumatra.

1825 Dadabhai Naoroji, born on 4 September, was the first Indian to be elected as a Member to the House of Commons in England, he was also a founding member of the Indian National Congress. All ring leaders of the Grenadier Company in Assam who refused to go on a march were sentenced to death. The first steamship, the Enterprise, took fifteen weeks to reach Calcutta from England, via the Cape of Good Hope.

1826 The first Indian Barrister, Gyanenda Mohan Tagore, was born on 24 January in Calcutta. Tea plants were found in Assam. Rubber plant seeds were first brought to India from Brazil.

1827 The first large scale strike was that of 2,900 palanquin bearers in Calcutta. Bengal Club was established.

1828 An army naturalist exploring coal in Assam came upon pockets of oil, however, he ignored them.

1829 New Regulations introduced state that anybody taking part in 'Suttee', the burning of Hindu widows, was to be charged with culpable homicide. East India Company founded the Indian Navy. Royal Calcutta Golf Club established.

1830 Ram Mohan Roy was the first Indian Brahmin to go to England. Iron and steel manufactured by modern methods in South Arcot in Madras. Bombay Public Library was opened. The first steam-driven paper-making machine set up in Calcutta.

1831 Thousands of 'Kols' were massacred when they revolted against their land being handed over to Sikh and Muslim farmers.

1832 British visit the Naga Hills to subdue the Nagas.

1833 Savings Bank facility was initiated. Ice imported for the first time when a shipload was sent from Boston, US to Calcutta. Ram Mohan Roy died on 27 September.

1834 Governor General William Bentinck changed the official language of the Courts of Justice from Persian to English.

1835 English language was introduced as the medium of instruction for higher studies. British King's image was put on Indian coins.

1836 Dwarkanath Gupta and Nobin Chandra Mitra dissected a dead body in Calcutta Medical College. The first public library, known as Calcutta Public Library, was opened.

1837 The first political organisation of India was the Zamindari Association of Calcutta. The first tea-estate was set up at Chabuwa in Assam by East India Co. Positive action initiated against human sacrifice in Orissa.

1838 The daily newspaper *Times of India* was published from Bombay. Indian emigration to the Caribbean.

1839 Calcutta Medical College Hospital opened for males only. The first electric telegraph line was installed from Calcutta to Diamond Harbour. Maharaja Ranjit Singh of Punjab died 27 June.

1840 Photographic cameras were introduced in Indian market.

1841 The first hospital for females opened in Calcutta.

1842 Lord Ellenborough returned the sandalwood gates of Somnath temple back from Ghazni.

1843 The legal status of slavery was abolished by the British.

1844 Bahai faith arrives in India from Iran.

1845 The first Hindi newspaper, the Benares Akhbar was published. The first Sikh war against the British started on 11 December. East India Company buys remaining Danish settlements in India.

1846 Lahore captured by the British.

1847 The Royal Calcutta Turf Club was established. The Nicobar Islands were abandoned by Denmark and offered for £50,000 to England which turned down the offer.

1848 The French abolished the slave trade in India.

1849 Second Anglo-Sikh war, the Sikhs were defeated, their kingdom ended and their army disbanded.

1850 The Kohinoor diamond, the fourth largest in the world, was taken from India and presented to Queen Victoria.

1851 Mancherjee Merwanjee Bhownaggree was born 27 August, he was elected a British Conservative Member of Parliament on 6 July,1895, one of only three Indians to become MPs when Britain had an Empire. The Geological Survey in India was established in Calcutta.

1852 The postal system for the general public was introduced in Karachi.

1853 Indian Railways started service from Bombay to Thana.

Competitive examination for the Indian Civil Service started in England. The first meteorological observation started in Calcutta.

1854 East India Railway ran its first passenger train between Calcutta and Hooghly. India's first modern post office was established. The first Indian textile mill was set up. The first Indian railway bridge was built to cross the Thana Creek in Bombay.

1855 The first long distance telegraph line was opened between Calcutta and Agra, it was 1,300 km. Armed Santhal revolt against British oppression and moneylenders was crushed leaving more than 15,000 Santhals dead and thousands homeless as many villages were destroyed. The first jute spinning mill was set up near Hooghly.

1856 Begum Hazrat Mahal, wife of Wajid Ali Shah the ruler of Oudh, organised a women's brigade and led her troops against the British dressed in the uniform of a male army officer. Law introduced authorising the remarriage of Hindu widows. The first widow marriage was arranged.

1857 The War of Independence first broke out in Bengal on 26 February in the 19th Bengal Infantry and on 17 May Bahadur Shah II was declared the independent Mughal Emperor of India. British recaptured Delhi on 20 September and the Emperor surrendered on 21 September. Calcutta had the first city gas pipeline for domestic cooking and street lighting. Calcutta, Bombay and Madras Universities were founded.

1858 J P Walker sailed from Calcutta with 200 mostly Sepoy prisoners to start a new settlement in the Andaman Islands, over 3,000 others would follow, never to return to the mainland. Transfer of authority from the East India Company to the British Crown. India became part of the British Empire on 1 November. The first two Indians were conferred with the Bachelor of Arts degrees from Calcutta University.

1859 Indigo riots started by Bengal peasants in protest against the torture and exploitation of the British Indigo planters.

1860 The Indian Penal Code (Act XLV) was passed into Law. The first batch of Indian 'contract' workers landed in South Africa. The keeping and trafficking of slaves made punishable crimes under the British Penal code. The world's first Polo Club was established at Silchar. Double-decker railway coaches introduced on the Bombay - Baroda route.

1861 Motilal Nehru was born 6 May at Agra. Rabindranath Tagore was born on 7 May. The first public auctions of tea were held in Calcutta. Polo Club established in Calcutta.

1862 Sambhunath Pandit was the first Indian to assume the office of the Judge of a High Court. Ganendra Mohan Tagore was the first Indian Barrister to be enrolled in Calcutta High Court. Bahadur Shah II, the last Mughal Emperor died in captivity, in Burma at age 87. The first industrial strike in India involved 1,200 railways workers at Howrah.

1863 Satyendra Prasanna Sinha was born 24 March, he was the first Indian to enter the Governor General's Executive Council and receive a peerage. The Indian Navy was transferred to the British Admiralty.

1865 Kathiwar State of Saurashtra was the first native State to issue its own postage stamp.

1866 Oil found on a commercial scale in Assam.

1867 The erection began of a seven-thousand mile telegraph line from London to Calcutta.

1868 Nicobar Islands were handed over to the British by the Danes - free of charge.

1869 Income Tax at the rate of one per cent was introduced. Mohandas Karamchand Gandhi was born on 2 October in Porbander, Gujarat and Kasturba, his wife-to-be, was also born in Porbander in the same year.

1870 Dada Saheb Phalke, the pioneer of Indian cinema, was born on 30 April. Phalke's role as Initiator of Cinematographic Art stands unrivalled in the history of Indian cinema. The first steamer from England via the Suez Canal reached India. Direct submarine cable line between India and England was established.

1871 The first national census in India figured the population at 206 million.

1872 Indians played football for the first time. Government of India passed the Native Marriage Act to legalise inter-religion and inter-caste marriages.

1874 Shapurji Saklatvala born 28 March, was to become the third Asian Member of the British parliament. Horse-drawn tramcars started running in Bombay. The first lady doctor Clara Swain, an American, came to India.

1875 Bombay Stock Exchange established on 9 July. The first Students' Union was founded. The first Zoological Gardens of India was founded in Calcutta. The Indian Meteorological Department was established. Snooker was first invented in Jabalpur by an army officer..

1876 The first night-school started for Bombay factory workers.

1877 Queen Victoria was proclaimed 'Queen and Empress of India'. Sir John Lawrence passenger steamer perished in a cyclone off Irissa coast on 25 May losing all 732 pilgrims on board including, 33 members of the same family.

1878 Calcutta University allowed women to appear in the Entrance Examination. The Siliguri-Darjeeling mountain train known as the 'Toy Train' started operating. Calcutta Museum opened to the public.

1879 C Rajagopalachariar, philosopher and nationalist leader was born on 10 December. Poetess and nationalist leader, Smt Sarojini Naidu, was born on 13 February. She was the first lady Governor of Uttar Pradesh. Bethune College of Calcutta was the only women's college in the British Empire outside Britain. Postcard of one pice was introduced by the Post and Telegraph Department.

1880 The first issue of *Illustrated Weekly of India*. Systematic exploitation of gold started in Kolar mines in Mysore. Hand-drawn rickshaw first appeared in Simla.

1881 Calcutta Homoeopathic Medical College was established. The first statue of an Indian, that of Ram Nath Tagore younger brother of Dwarkanath Tagore, was unveiled in Calcutta. Calcutta gets its first horse-drawn tramcar and India's first telephone exchange.

1882 The Postal Savings Bank system was introduced on 1 April. A cow protection association was formed which led to communal problems.

1883 India's first public theatre hall opened in Calcutta. Kadambini Ganguli and Chandramukhi Basu were the first two Indian women to pass BA examinations from Calcuuta University. Kadambini Ganguli was to became the first Indian female doctor in 1888. Gandhi marries.

1885 The Indian National Congress held its first meeting in Bombay Tejpal Hall. The Bombay Institute for Deaf and Mute was established.

1886 Rash Behari Bose, the great revolutionary, was born on 25 May. Dr S Muthulakshmi Reddi was born on 30 July, she had many firsts to her name including being the first woman Deputy President of a Legislature in the world. Sri Ramakrishna Paramahansa Dev died on 16 August. Raja Mahendra Pratap, who had escaped from India in 1914 to become the Head of the provisional Indian Government in Kabul, returned to India after 31 years of self-exile. The first Indian cricket team toured England.

1887 Gandhi sailed for Great Britain. The first National Chamber of Commerce, the Bengal Chamber of Commerce was established. The first School for the Blind was established in Dehradun.

1888 The first houseboat *Victory* was built at Dal lake in Srinagar. Gandhi sailed to England to study law.

1889 The first All Indian Football Tournament. British India Committee was opened in London. The first successful oil well was sunk at Digboi. Jawaharlal Nehru, India's first Prime Minister was born on 14 November. Smt Bidhu Mukhi and Smt Mary Virginia Mitter were the first two females get a Bachelor of Medicine degree.

1890 Ram Chandra Chatterjee was the first person to make a descent by parachute from a hot air balloon at Calcutta on 22 March. The bicycle made its first appearance in India.

1891 Bhimji Ramji Ambedkar was born ('untouchable') on 14 April. He was the prime architect of the Constitution of Independent India and known as 'the father of the Indian constitution'. India's population according to recent census was 279,446,000. Gandhi became a Barrister.

1892 The first automobile was imported by Maharaja of Patiala.

1893 Gandhi sailed to South Africa to join Law practice.

1894 The first Philatelic exhibition was held in Calcutta. The first Indian bank, Punjab National Bank, was opened.

1895 Vinayak Narahari Bhave was born on 11 September, he was Gandhi's staunchest spiritual heir He was a freedom fighter who was sent to prison many times. Prince Ranjit Singhji was the first Indian to play in English County Cricket. The first railway steam engine was built. Wireless signals were successfully transmitted by J C Bose, one year before Marconi.

1896 Cinema came to India when a team of French agents from Lumiere Brothers began showing short titles.

1897 Netaji Subhas Chandra Bose was born on 23 January. The great nationalist leader escaped from India to fight against the British in the Second World War. The world's first fingerprint bureau was set up in Calcutta. Malaria parasites were discovered in Calcutta. The first poor-house was set up in Darjeeling. Zakir Hussain, India's third president was born on 8 February.

1898 Damodar Hari Chapekar was the first Indian freedom fighter to hang as a terrorist, he shot the plague commissioner and magistrate of Pune. The first Indian music was produced on gramophone record in a Belighata factory.

1899 Calcutta received the first supply of electric current. Harischandra Bhatvadekar was the first Indian to make a film.

1900 Shrimati Vijayalakshmi Pandit, the first female President of the UNO General Assembly, was born on 18 August. The first rubber plantation was set up in Kerala. India had its first electric tram. Norman Pritchard was the first Indian to win an Olympic medal.

1901 Smt. Kadambini Ganguli was the first Indian female to address the Indian National Congress at Calcutta. Gandhi attended the Indian National Congress session for the first time. The Indian Ladies Magazine, India's first women's magazine published.

1902 Madame Bhikaiji Rustam K R Cama carried her message of freedom against British rule to America and Europe She was known as the "Mother of Indian Revolution". The first Indian, Miss Sashimuhk of Calcutta, recorded a song.

1903 King Edward VII was declared Emperor of India. Gandhi started a legal practice and the British Indian Association in South Africa. The Taj Mahal Hotel was opened in Bombay.

1904 The first Sikh migrants went to Canada.

1905 First partition of Bengal. Indian National Congress declared boycott of British goods in protest against partition.

1906 The earliest tri-colour flag was green and yellow with red stripes and seven lotuses. All India Muslim League was formed.

1907 Electric tram introduced into Bombay. Bhagat Singh threw a bomb in the Central Assembly in Delhi. The Gandhi cap became one of the great symbols of freedom fighters in India. First two Indians were admitted to Privy Council of India. The first cinema opened in Calcutta. Jim Corbett shot the Champawat tigress in Kumoan region, which had caused 436 human deaths.

1908 Khudiram Bose, at age 19, was the youngest to die on the gallows for freedom of India. The Calcutta Stock Exchange opened. Bal Gangadhar Tilak, considered Father of India's Freedom Struggle, was exiled for sedition, for six-years in Mandalay, Burma.

1909 Madan Lal was hanged in Pentonville prison, London, England. He was the first Indian revolutionary to be hanged in the UK for political killings. Gandhi sailed from South Africa to put India's case to British government.

1910 Mother Teresa born on 26 August to an Albanian family in Skopje, Macedonia.

1911 The world's first official airmail flight was made by Frenchman, Henri Pequet, in a Humber Sommer biplane, on 18 February between Bamrauli near Allahabad and Naina. The distance of six miles across the Ganges took 13 minutes. King George V and Queen Mary are the first ever British monarchy to land in Bombay. The Imperial capital of India moved from Calcutta to Delhi. 'Jana, Gana, Mana' India's national anthem first sung on 27 December at the Indian National Congress session in Calcutta.

1912 A bomb was exploded to disrupt the initiation of Delhi as the newly appointed capital. Horses were brought from Australia for the Mounted Police Force formed in Calcutta.

1913 Rabindranath Tagore was the first Indian to be awarded the Nobel Prize for literature. The first automatic telephone system was installed at Shimla with 700 lines.

1914 First World War starts. *S S Komagata Maru* sailed from Hong Kong to Vancouver with Sikh and Punjabi Muslim protesters to challenge the colour bar in Canada. Gandhi leaves South Africa for India.

1915 Gandhi returns to Bombay from South Africa. Rabindranath Tagore gets Knighthood from the British Government. The Provisional Government of India was established in exile in Kabul.

1916 The Zoological Survey was established on 2 July.

1917 Indira Gandhi was born on 19 November. The demand for reorganisation of States on linguistic basis first originated. Mrs Annie Besant was the first woman to head the Indian National Congress as President. Women's Indian Association was established by her.

1918 Indra Lal Roy was the first pilot to get the Distinguished Flying Cross. He was the first ace pilot to shoot down nine German planes and who was later killed in an air battle over London. Smt. Nanibala Debi was the first female political prisoner of the modern period. The great influenza epidemic took a heavy toll throughout the world and affected 5 million people in India. First World War ends.

1919 As the result of an attack on an English school teacher, the infamous 'crawling and flogging order' was issued. 379 people were killed and 1,208 wounded when Brig, Gen. Dyer opened fire on an unarmed assembly of people in Jallianwala Bagh in Amristar, Punjab. RabindranathTagore renunciated his Knighthood in protest at the massacre.

1920 Organised air transport began in India with two Royal Air Force planes between Bombay and Karachi. Ravi Shankar Bhattacharya was born on 7 April. Future Prime Minister P.V. Narasimha Rao was born on 28 June. Communist Party of India was formed at Tashkent on 17 October. The inaugural session of the All India Trade Union Congress

was held in Bombay. Gandhi started to work against 'untouchability'. Gandhi also joined the All India Home Rule League and become its President. India participated in the Olympic games

1921 The Indian National Congress flag was adopted. Mopla (Muslim) Revolt was started in Malabar. Gandhi made a bonfire of British clothes and resolved to wear only a loin cloth to propagate homespun cotton and signify his identification with the people. India participated in the Davis Cup Tournament. Imperial Bank of India was started, later named State Bank of India.

1922 Gandhi arrested for the first time in India on 10 March. Sentenced to six years on charge of sedition for articles that appeared in the weekly newspaper *Young India* of which he was the editor

1923 Smt. Cornelia Sorabji became the first woman advocate.

1924 Open competitive examination started for recruitment of Indians into Indian Police Service.

1925 The first electric train service started between Bombay and Kurla. First family planning clinic opened in Bombay.

1926 Jim Corbett killed notorious man-eating leopard of Rudraprayag area. The leopard created a reign of terror between 1918 and 1926 having killed 125 people. Trade Union Act was passed. Indian cricket team played their first unofficial cricket Test match. Bus service introduced in Calcutta.

1927 Sarat Kumar Roy was the first Asian to go to the North Pole.

1928 India wins Olympic Gold Medal in Hockey. Judo introduced into India.

1929 JRD Tata was the first Indian to secure a pilot's licence. The first commercial passenger service was the Indian State Air Services owned by the Government of India. Lata Mangeshkar, the great playback movie singer, held the unique world record of 30,000 gramophone records to her credit. Joan Page, an English lady, was the first woman to fly an airplane in Calcutta. Miss Jennifer Sandeson, an Anglo-Indian, was the first woman participant in Wimbledon Tennis Tournament. Mother Teresa came to India and settled in Calcutta. Airmail stamp was issued for the first time.

1930 Gandhi started Civil Disobedience Movement and commenced his Dandi march for 'Salt Satyagraha'. He was arrested and jailed without trial. 100,000 persons arrested. Surya Sen alias Masterda and his 62 men of the Indian Republican Army raided Chittagong armoury and aroused great national aspirations throughout India. The first deluxe train was introduced. C.V. Raman got the Nobel Prize in Physics. Bhagat Lal was the first pilot trained in India. Age of Consent Act raises marriageable age for girls to 14 years and to 18 years for boys.

1931 The capital of India moved from Old Delhi to New Delhi on 10 February. Winston Churchill described Gandhi as a 'half naked seditious fakir'. Indian Air Force came into existence. Bata India started shoe manufacture in West Bengal.

1932 Indian cricket team played the first official Test at Lords, England. India's first airliner service started between Bombay and Karachi on 15 October. The All India Harijan Sevak Sangh for social reform and education of the depressed class was founded. Gandhi begins fast unto death, while in prison, in protest at British introduction of separate electorate for 'Untouchables'.

1933 Indian National Airways started India's first daily passenger air service.

1934 The great earthquake of Bihar claims 20,000 lives.

1935 Reserve Bank of India came into existence. Doon School of Dehradun, was established as India's first public school.

Gandhi retired from Indian National Congress and politics in order to devote himself to village welfare.

1936 Shakuntala Devi, the human calculating machine was born on 4 November. All government temples in Kerala were opened to all Hindus, irrespective of their caste. Vijayalakshmi Pandit became the first woman Cabinet Minister. King George V dies.

1937 Burma separated from India.

1938 The first bicycle industry set up in Calcutta. Employment of Children Act passed.

1939 Second World War starts in Europe

1940 Former Governor of Punjab shot dead in London in a belated political revenge attack for the 1919 Amritsar massacre. Civil disobedience campaign against Britian's refusal to allow Indians to express their opinions regarding World War Two. 23,000 arrested within a year.

1941 Rabindranath Tagore dies on 7 August. Japan entesr war and bombs Pearl Harbour.

1942 Japanese Navy and Air Force touched Port Blair, took control of Singapore and bombed India. During the mass upheaval called 'August Movement' 1,028 killed, 3.125 seriously injured, 60,000 people were arrested, 26,000 convicted and 18,000 detained under the Defence of India Act. The first motor car manufacturing unit was incorporated in Calcutta. India's first blood bank was opened. Indian National Army was formed in Malaya and consisted of 50,000 officers and soldiers, who had surrendered to the Japanese.

1943 The only daylight air-raid on Calcutta by the Japanese took place on 5 December. Dr. M C Mody operated on 833 cataract patients at a stretch, a world record. (By 1989 he had performed 595,019 further operations). Indian National Army handed over to Subhas Chandra Bose, former President of the Indian Congress who inaugurated the Government of Free India in Singapore.

1944 Kasturba Gandhi, Gandhi's wife died in internment age 74, in Aga Khan Palace in Pune. An exploded ammunition ship, the *SS Fort Stikine*, took 1,200 lives and 45 days to contain the conflagration. Gandhi was named 'Father of the Nation' after spending 2,089 days in Indian prisons and 249 days in South African prisons.

1945 Indian National Army surrenders after the collapse of Japan. Indian National Army prisoners tried for treason at the Red Fort, Delhi. Second World War ends.

1946 Demonstrations against trial of INA men. Indian soldiers refused to fire on the 1,100 naval ratings and 30,000 other ratings who went on strike to protest about low pay. As a result of a call for 'Direct Action Day' on 16 August, by the Muslim League riots break out. The 'Calcutta killings' took a toll of 5,000 lives with 15,000 injured and more than 100,000 rendered homeless.

1947 British Prime Minister announced that the British would leave India. India's National Flag was adopted by Constituent Assembly. India partitioned into India and Pakistan. India was declared independent on 15 August. Pandit Jawaharlal Nehru was the first Prime Minister of free India. The Constitution of India was finalised in November and came into force in January 1950. The first post-independence postage stamp issued and Reserve Bank of India nationalised.

1948 Gandhi ended his seventeenth and last fast on 18 January. He was assassinated on 30 January, on what is now called Martyrs' Day, he was in his 79th year. The last British soldiers left India on 28 February. Air India International was established. C. Rajagopalachari became the first and only Indian Governor General of India, as well as being the last Governor General. All discriminations against women in employment were removed. Employees' State Insurance Act was passed. West Indies cricket team first visited India. Mother Teresa became an Indian citizen. The first India-made motor car came off the assembly line.

1949 Hindi declared the National Language of India. The Constitution of India was adopted on 26 November. Women were inducted in the Calcutta Police Force.

1950 'Jana Gana Mana...' became the National Anthem. Rajendra Prasad was elected the first President. India made into a Sovereign Democratic Republic on January 26. A replica of the Lion Capital of Ashoka's pillar at Sarnath, became the Indian National Emblem. Supreme Court of India was inaugurated. Mother Teresa founded 'Missionaries of Charity'. Dilip Bose the first Indian to be seeded in the Wimbledon Tennis Championship, he was ranked 16th.

1951 Prem Mathur was the first woman pilot to get a commercial pilot's licence. The first census of free India revealed 720 languages, fourteen major tongues and over 2,300 recognised castes, creeds and sects. Eleven countries and 489 males and females participated in the first Asian Games held in Delhi. The first aircraft designed and manufactured in India makes its maiden flight. Except for a few minor private sector companies, Indian railways were nationalised. Monotosh Roy was declared Mr Universe. The first police dog squad was set up in Madras.

1952 The first International Film Festival was opened in Bombay. India has its first cricket Test victory. Saifuddin Kitchlu was the first Indian to get Lenin Peace Prize. The world's first official Family Planning Programme was launched. Monohar Aich became Mr Universe in short height category in London. K D Yadav won Bronze Medal wrestling at Bantam weight to gain India's first official Olympic medal in athletics. Indian cricket team visited West Indies for the first time. Pakistan cricket team visited India for the first time.

1953 Mount Everest was conquered for the first time by Sherpa Tenzing Norgay and Edmund Hillary. All airlines of India were nationalised. Valerian Gracias was the first Indian to be appointed as a Cardinal.

1954 National Film Award was introduced. Indian cricket team visited Pakistan for the first time.

1955 India's first newsprint factory started production. Untouchability (Offence) Act came into force. Manufacture of motorcycles, scooters and three-wheelers started. Hindu Marriage Act fixed the minimum age for girls at 15 years and boys at 18 years, it also provided for divorce and judicial separation. New Zealand cricket team visited India for the first time. National Leprosy Eradication Programme started.

1956 2,500th anniversary of Buddha's birth. Hindu Succession Act was passed. Ashoka Hotel was the first 5-star deluxe hotel to be opened in India. Indian States were reorganised on linguistic basis. Nehru, Tito and Nasser work to found the Non-Aligned Movement. Australian cricket team visited India for the first time. BR Ambedkar died 6 December.

1957 India's first atomic research reactor was inaugurated. Sarah Cherian became the Mayor of Madras Corporation and thus the first woman Mayor in India.

1957 Second General Election. Rajendra Prasad elected Head of State for second term.

1958 The Copyright Bill was passed. Metric system of weights and measures introduced.

1959 Dalai Lama XIV fled from Tibet to reach India on 17 March and was given political asylum. The first successful open heart surgery was performed on a twelve-year old girl. Arati Saha was the first Asian female to swim the English Channel. Dwight D Eisenhower become the first US president to visit India. Gita Chanda became the first woman paratrooper.

1960 Air India introduces service to London and New York becoming the first Asian country to operate over the Atlantic. Subscriber Trunk Dialling STD was introduced between Kanpur and Lucknow. Manuel Aaron became India's first International Master in chess. Diners' Club International introduces credit cards into India. Bombay divided into Maharashtra and Gujarat States.

1961 Madras State was renamed Tamil Nadu. India's first aircraft carrier commissioned. The first India-made supersonic fighter took to the air. Government of India took military action which led to the liberation of Goa after more than 450 years of colonial rule. Maternity Benefit Act was introduced for married women employees.

1962 Third General Election. War with China on India's northern border. Birla Planetarium in Calcutta was the first one in Asia - seating 689. Ceasefire declared by China.

1963 The first National Library for the Blind was set up. India's space programme began. Nagaland became the 16th State of India. Rajendra Prasad dies.

1964 The first Vintage Car Rally was organised in Calcutta. Jawaharlal Nehru, India's first Prime Minister, died on 27 May and his ashes were strewn over the Himalayas. Mrigthuni peak at 22,490 feet, was climbed by the first Indian women-only expedition. The first Papal visit to India was made by Pope Paul VI.

1965 On 9 April fighting broke out between Indian and Pakistani troops. The first Indian team ascended Mount Everest, this expedition included Sherpa Nawang Gombu who reached the summit for the second time - the first man in the world to do so. India's first eye bank was opened in Calcutta Medical College Hospital.

1966 Indira Gandhi became the third Prime Minister of India. The Guinness Book of Records hailed Mihir Sen as a unique long distance swimmer as a result of his many remarkable swimming feats. Rupee was devalued by 36.5 per cent. Rita Faria, a medical student, was elected 'Miss World' in London. The States of Harayana and Punjab come into being.

1967 Fourth General Election. Indira Gandhi became Indian Prime Minister for a second time. Dr Zakir Hussain elected President. Nagaland adopted English as the official language of State. India Tourism Development Corporation Ltd was set up.

1968 Dr Prafulla Kumar Sen and others performed the first heart transplantation in Bombay, he was the third surgeon in the world to do so. Hargovind Khorana, an American citizen, was the third Indian to get the Nobel Prize. India's first meteorological rocket was launched.

1969 The first Superfast Express train was introduced between New Delhi and Howrah. India's first atomic power station at Tarapore became operational. Apollo 11 crew visit Bombay. Gir forest, the last remaining habitat of the Asian lion, was established as a reserve. Madras State renamed Tamil Nadu.

1970 The first woman career-diplomat was appointed Ambassador to Hungary. The first Sewage Water Reclamation Plant of India for commercial use was commissioned. Indian Air Force got the first India-made supersonic MIG-21 combat aircraft. Haryana become the first State to achieve hundred per cent electrification. State of Meghalaya comes into being.

1971 Himachal Pradesh becomes a State. India established the first satellite communication link. Air India's first Jumbo jet landed at Bombay. Indo-Pakistan war broke out again, as a result East Pakistan emerged as a sovereign independent country, Bangladesh. Medical Termination of Pregnancy Act was passed by Government.

1972 India produced world record 433 feature films in 1971. National memorial 'Amar Jawan' was installed in New Delhi. The first World Book Fair was inaugurated in New Delhi. Postal Index Number of 6-digits introduced. Wildlife Preservation Act passed to protect various species from extinction including tigers and lions. Tiger chosen as India's National Animal. Work started on Metro Railway in Calcutta. Indira Gandhi received the highest civilian award, the 'Bharat Ratna'.

1973 All non-coking coal mines were nationalised. The first all-

women police station was set at Calicut. India's first International Philatelic Exhibition was opened in New Delhi. Govind Das, MP, completed 50 years as a Parliamentarian. Project Tiger was initiated to protect tigers whose numbers had dropped to1,827 in a 1972 census. Mysore changes its name to Karnataka.

1974 India's first nuclear detonation took place underground in the Rajasthan desert at a depth of 107 metres.

1975 India declared as one of the countries in the world to eradicate smallpox. India accords recognition to Palestine Liberation Organisation India's first satellite, designed by the Indian Space Research Organisation, was launched on 19 April. Durba Banerjee became the first female pilot in the world to command a commercial passenger flight. President declares a State of Emergency. 'Bonded' labour abolished by Ordinance .

1976 The lost city of Kapilavastu, where Gautam Buddha spent 29 years of his life, was found in an excavation. Four Indians successfully skied down the slopes of Trishul Peak (7,120 metres) putting India on top of the world's ski map. Major-General Gertrude Ali Ram was the first woman General in the Indian Army. International Direct Dialing telephone link was established.

1977 India's Naval Coastguard established. First Indian wins both the World Amateur and Open Billiards Championship in Melbourne with a break of 1,149. The first statue of an Indian woman, Matangini Hazra, was unveiled in Calcutta. Pet-named Ghandi Buri, the 72 year-old widow was shot in Tamluk, while leading the Congress procession as standard bearer, during the August Movement. Sanjivam Reddi elected President.

1978 India's first double-decker train makes its maiden run. The Child Marriage Act amended marriageable age for girls to 18 years and boys to 21. India's first and the world's second test tube baby was born. Fifteen year-old Rohini Khadikar become the first woman to win the National Chess Championship.

1979 India's first Jumbo passenger train, the Tamil Nadu Express travelled from Delhi to Madras. The world's largest ever cheque in banking history of Rs16,640 million was handed over to India by the US ambassador. Morarji Desai was the first Indian Prime Minister to resign. Mother Teresa got the Nobel Prize for peace. India's seventh general election held.

1980 Sanjay Gandhi the younger son of Indira Gandhi, who led the Youth Congress, died in a plane crash. Oil was struck in the Bay of Bengal. The first experimental colour telecast was made from Madras TV Centre. Mother Teresa awarded Bharat Ratna India's highest national award.

1981 India became the seventh nation to develop collecting polymetallic nodules. The first night-time cricket match was played in Bombay on 10 May. 'Rent-A-Car' system setup in India. Central Bank of India was the first Indian bank to introduce Credit Cards. Khalistan activists hijack Indian Airlines Boeing 737.

1982 Mahatma Gandhi Road Bridge across the Ganga at Patna was, at 5,575 metres, the longest bridge built on a river. India's first telecast in colour was shown. Regular colour telecasting started from Delhi. The Ninth Asian Games started.

1983 India took leadership of the seventh Non-Aligned Summit for the first time. The first pilotless plane was tested near Kolar. India's unique three-in-one satellite INSAT-1B was deployed from American space shuttle to orbit at 35,680 km above the earth. Bhanu Athaiya was the first Indian to win an Oscar Award for costume design in the film *Gandhi*. The film won eight Oscar Awards.

1984 Squadron Leader Rakesh Sharma was the first Indian to go into space. Captain H.J. Singh created a world high altitude hang-gliding record. On the 5 May, Phu Dorji was the first Indian to climb Mount Everest without oxygen. Bachendri

Krishna: Myths, Rights and Attitudes	M. Singer, Princeton University Press
Manual of Hindu Astrology, A	B. V. Raman, IBH Prakashana, Bangalore
Muslims: Their Religious Beliefs and Practices	Andrew Rippin, Routledge
Parsis, The: Essays on their Sacred Language, Writings and Religion	Martin Haug, Cosmo Publications
Sadhus: Holy Men of India	Dolf Hartsuiker, Thames and Hudson
Sikh Concept of the Divine	Pritam Singh, ed., Guru Nanak Dev University Press
Sikhs: Their Religious Beliefs and Practices, The	W. O. Cole and P. Singh Sambhi, Routledge
Understanding the Muslim Mind	Rajmohan Gandhi, Penguin
Yodacara Idealism, The	Ashok Kumar Chatterjee, Motilal Banarsidass
Yonitantra, The	J. A. Schoterman, ed., Manohar Publications
Zoroastrians: Their Religious Beliefs and Practices	Mary Boyce, Routledge

SOCIETY AND CULTURE

Andamanese, Nicobarese and Hill Tribes of Assam, The	A. M. Meerwarth, Spectrum Publications, Calcutta
Anglo-Indian Attitudes: The Mind of the Indian Civil Service	Clive Dewey, The Hambledon Press
Biography of Bombay, A	Gillian Tindall, Temple Smith
Bombay in Transition	Meera Kosambi, Almqvist & Wiksell International, Stockholm
Bonded Labour in India	Sarma Marla, Biblia Impex Private Ltd., New Delhi
Calcutta: The City Revealed	Geoffrey Moorhouse, Penguin Books
Caste Among Non-Hindus in India	Harjinder Singh, National Publishing House
Caste and Class in India	G. S. Ghurye, Popular Book Depot, Bombay
Caste and Race in India	G. S. Ghurye, Popular Prakashan (5th ed.)
Caste and Social Stratification among Muslims in India	Imtiaz Ahmad, ed., South Asia Books
Child Labour in India	Dr. M. K. Pandhe, ed., India Book Exchange, Calcutta
City of Gold	Gillain Tindall, Penguin
Civilisation of India, The	R. C. Dutt, Routledge and Kagan Paul
Customs & Etiquette in India	Venika Kingsland, Globa Books Ltd.
Delhi: A Portrait	Kushwant Singh and Raghu Rai, Oxford University Press
Delhi Through Ages	R. E. Frykenberg, Oxford University Press
Dharma's Daughters	Sara Mitter, Penguin
Dynamics of Santal Traditions in a Peasant Society	George E. Somers, Abinhav Publications, New Delhi
Dynamics of Tribal Development	Pradip Kumar Bhowmick, Inter-India Publications, New Delhi
Encyclopedia of Indian Culture	Sterling Publishers Private Ltd.
Family, Kinship and Marriage in India	Dr. Patricia Uberoi, ed., Oxford University Press
Frogs in a Well	Patricia Jeffrey, Zed Press
From the Vedas to the Manusamhita: A Cultural Study	Vibhuti Bhushan Mishra, Sterling Publishers Private Ltd.
Furies of Indian Communalism, The	Achin Vanaik, Verso
Future of India, The	R. Coupland, Oxford University Press
Hindu Castes and Sects	J. N. Bhatacharya (reprinted in 1968)
Hindu Social Organisation	P. H. Prabhu, Popular Prakashan, Bombay
Hindu Society: An Interpretation	Iravati Karve, Deshmuk Prakashan
Idea of India, The	Sunil Khilnani, Hamish Hamilton
India: A Socio-Economic Profile	Brij Raj Chauhan
India File	Trevor Fishlock, John Murray Publishers Ltd.
India 1995	Ministry of Information and Broadcasting, Government of India
Indian Dimension, The: The Indian Family in Transition	John S. Augustine, Vikas Publishing House Pvt. Ltd.
Indian Social Scene: Evils and Remedies	Navin Chandra Joshi, Uma Joshi, Deep and Deep Publications
India Who's Who	Infa Publications, New Delhi
India's Bandit Queen: The True Story of Phoolan Devi	Mala Sen, Harvill (an imprint of HarperCollins Publishers)
Khasi Canvas, The	J. N. Chowdhury, Srimati Jaya Chowdhury, Shillong
Language and Society in Modern India	Robert I. Crane and Bradford Spangenberg, eds., Heritage
Living City, The, Volume I, The Past	Sukanta Chaudhuri, ed., University of Oxford Press
Living City, The, Volume II, The Present & Future	Sukanta Chaudhuri, ed., University of Oxford Press

May You Be the Mother of a Hundred Sons	Elizabeth Bumiller, Penguin
National and Left Movements in India	K. N. Panikkar, ed., Vikas Publishing House Pvt. Ltd.
New Horizons and Scheduled Castes	C. Parvathamma and SatyanarayanaAshish Publishing House
New Moon	Anees Jung, Penguin
No Full Stops in India	Mark Tully, Viking/Penguin Group
Origin of Bombay, The	J. Gerson Da Cunha, Asian Educational Services, New Delhi
Philosophies of India	H. Zimmer, Pantheon Books
Plain Tales from the Raj	Charles Allen, Abacus Travel
Politics of Continental Development	Ramesh Thapar, Vikas Publishing House Pvt. Ltd.
Politics of Sikh Separatism, The	Rajiv A Kapur, Allen & Unwin
Religion and Society in the Brahma Purana	Surabhi Sheth, Sterling Publishers Private Ltd.
Rumour of Calcutta, The	John Hutnyk, Zed Books
Rural India in Transition	A. R. Desai, Popular Prakashan, Mumbai
Social Change in Modern India	M. N. Srinivas, University of California Press
Social Reform, Sexuality and the State	Dr. Patricia Uberoi, ed., Sage Publications, New Delhi
Soul of India, The	A. De Reincourt, Sterling Publishers/Honeyglen Publishers
Sources of Indian Tradition: Volume II Modern India	Stephen Hay, ed., Penguin
Surplus Labour and the City: A Study of Bombay	Heather and Vijay Joshi, Oxford University Press
Tribes of India - The Struggle for Survival	Christoph von Fuerer-Haimendorf, Oxford University Press
Tribes of Assam	S. Barkataki, National Book Trust, India
Tribal Heritage of India	S. C. Dube, ed., Vikas Publishing House Pvt. Ltd., New Delhi
Tribal Social Change in India	K. L. Lothari, Hinanshu Publications, New Delhi
Untouchables in Contemporary India, The	J. M. Mahar, ed., University of Arizona Press
Unveiling India	Anees Jung, Penguin
We, the People	Nani. A. Palkhivala, Strand Book Stall
Wonder That Was India, The	A. L. Basham, Sedgwick & Jackson

TRAVEL

Chasing the Monsoon	Alexander Frazer, Penguin India
David Gentleman's India	A John Curtis Book, Hodder and Stoughton Ltd.
Goddess in Stones, A	Norman Lewis, Pan Macmillan
Great Railway Bazaar, The	Paul Theroux, Penguin
India by Rail	Royston Ellis, Bradt (Chalfont St. Peter, Bucks)
India File	Trevor Fishlock, Rupa, New Delhi
India: Land of Dreams and Fantasy	Doranne Jacobson, W H Smith Ltd.
India; A Literary Companion	Bruce Palling, John Murray (Publishers) Ltd.
India Travel Atlas	Lonely Planet Publications
India - Travel Survival Kit	Lonely Planet Publications
India You Do Not Know, The	P. N. Chopra and Prabha Chopra, eds., Sterling Publishers
Insight Guide: India	APA Productions
Into India	John Keay, John Murray Publishers Ltd.
Journey Through India, A	Lustre Press Pvt. Ltd.
Let's Go: India and Nepal	Let's Go Publications, Macmillan
Lonely Planet Travel Atlas: India	Lonely Planet Publications
Museums of India	Shobita Punja, The Guidebook Company Ltd., Hong Kong
Portable India, A	Jug Surarya and Anurag Mathur, eds., Harper Collins India
Royal Palaces of India, The	George Michell and Antonio Martinelli, Thames and Hudson
Three-quarters of a footprint	Joe Roberts, Transworld Publishers Ltd.

WILDLIFE

Birds of the Indian Subcontinent	Bikram Grewal, Guidebook Company Ltd., Hong Kong
Book of Indian Animals, The	S. H. Prater, Oxford University Press
Book of Indian Birds, The	Salim Ali, Natural History Society, Bombay
Book of Indian Reptiles, The	J. C. Daniel, Oxford University Press
Domestic Animals	Harbans Singh, National Book Trust, India
Insight Indian Wildlife Guide	APA Productions

Credits

WRITERS

BHIKHU PAREKH	INDIA'S DIVERSITY
I. N. CHOUDHURI	RELIGIONS OF INDIA
GONASEELAN GOVENDER	THE LONG MARCH TO FREEDOM
KEITH BENNETT	1947-1997: A FLEETING MOMENT IN THE LIFE OF A TIMELESS NATION
T. K. ARUN	INDIA: FIFTY YEARS INTO THE FUTURE
AMALENDU MISRA	A TALE OF THREE CITIES
MALA THAPAR	FAMILY STRUCTURES; WOMEN IN INDIA; THE TRIBAL PEOPLES
PATRICIA UBEROI	MARRIAGE
JASLEEN DHAMIJA	THE SARI
DEVENDRA CHINTAN	THE CASTE SYSTEM
RASHME SEHGAL	INDIAN DANCE; AN EVOCATION OF THE DIVINE: INDIA'S TIMELESS MUSICAL TRADITION
RASHEED TALIB	MEDIA AND SOCIETY: THE LATEST REVOLUTION
ANIL THAPAR	A WORLD OF ADVENTURE
ADAM LICUDI	A PASSION FOR CRICKET
T. HARIDAS	FOOD
DIPTA SEN	ASSAM; THE NORTH EAST STATES; WEST BENGAL
SUKHUMAR MURALIDHARAN	KARNATAKA; KERALA; TAMIL NADU
KUSHWANT SINGH	PUNJAB
JOHN HUGHES	NOTABLE EVENTS IN INDIA'S HISTORY

PHOTOGRAPHY:

PRINCIPAL PHOTOGRAPHY	PANKAJ SHAH
PICTURE EDITOR & CAPTIONS	PAUL FRASER

ADDITIONAL PHOTOGRAPHY:

AMLAN PALIWAL	Inside Front Cover, 256
FRANK KRAHMER	18
RESOURCE PHOTO	16, 130, 197, 199 - 205, 232
NAVNIT DHOLAKIA	117
ILAY COOPER	136 - Tribal Cloth
AVINASH PASRICHA	136 - Rock Garden, 149
ANIL A DAVE	139
JOHN WORRAL	141 - Haveli door
JOHN HUGHES	150, 151, 152
RAGHUBIR SINGH	162, 240, 246, 305, 322
NORMA JOSEPH	236, 238, 239
MAURICE JOSEPH	243, 278
CHRIS CALDICOTT	244
IAN CUMING	262
GERALD CUBIT	294
JAGDISH YADAV	286 - Imphal, 290, 292
MADAN ARORA	296, 329
DILIP MEHTA/COLOROFIC	304

PAGE 138 PHOTOGRAPHS COURTESY OF ANNA MARIA & FABIO ROSSI
PEACOCK ILLUSTRATION ON PAGE 14 COURTESY OF MYSTERIES OF INDIA
(0181 - 574 2727)

PREVIOUS PAGE: *A sari maker in West Bengal*

OPPOSITE: **DEVAPRAYAG**, *a holy site in Uttar Pradesh, is at the confluence of the Bhagirathi and Alaknanda rivers, forming the Ganga. The sacred* **GANGA** *starts its 2,525-kilometres journey to the Bay of Bengal from an icy cave of the Gangotri glacier called Gamukh (Cow's Mouth) in the Western Himalayas, 4,000 metres above sea level and more than two hundred kilometres away. This is the major river of the Indian subcontinent and is India's lifeline. Its basin, one of the most fertile and populated regions in the world, spreads across eight States. The Ganga irrigates up to 47 percent of the country and has been the main channel of communications and trade since ancient times. It is threatened by pollutants, industrial effluents, toxins from chemical fertilisers, pesticides, and millions of litres of sewage each day. The Ganga Action Plan launched in 1985 was the largest ever river clean-up operation, but proved ineffective. A new plan formulated in 1995 and called the National River Action Plan (NRAP) established sewage treatment plants.*

Other titles from Hansib

NAOROJI: THE FIRST ASIAN MP
A biography of Dadabhai Naoroji: Indian Patriot and British Liberal
OMAR RALPH
The life of the 'Grand Old Man of India' and the first non-European member of the British Parliament. This book charts his story from a humble beginning in Bombay, to the time when he saw the foundations of modern India laid down. Unfortunately, he has not been remembered by many people, although he died within living memory, in 1917, and was a mentor to men such as Gandhi.
Illustrated with rare black and white photographs
Paperback ISBN 976-8163-05-4 £11.95

BHOWNAGGREE
Member of Parliament 1895-1906
JOHN R HINNELLS AND OMAR RALPH
A biography of Sir Mancherjee Merwanjee Bhownaggree, Conservative MP for Bethnal Green, London, at the turn of the century. Much maligned in his day for allegedly forgetting his Indian heritage, his life and work as an MP in Britain and as an Indian statesman is now being re-assessed. This book was published to mark the parliamentary centenary of the first Asian Conservative MP.
Paperback ISBN 1-870518-48-9 £3

CORNERED TIGERS
A history of Pakistan's Test cricket
ADAM LICUDI WITH WASIM RAJA
The first ever authoritative history of Pakistani Test cricket, from its beginning in 1952 to the present by the former sports editor of the Asian Times, assisted by former Test star, Wasim Raja. With a unique collection of profiles from Abdul Hafeez Kardar, the first captain, to the giants of today, Wasim Akram, Waqar Younis and Inzamam-ul-Haq. This exciting and diligently researched book also honours Tigers like Hanif Mohammad, Fazal Mahmood, Imran Khan and Javed Miandad. Never before has there been so meticulous a chronicle of the highs and lows, the dramas and traumas of one of the greatest cricketing teams of all time with a sublime individual and collective talent.
Includes full scorecards from every Pakistan Test match and Test and One-Day averages for every Pakistan player.
Paperback ISBN 1-870518-31-4 £16.95

WOMEN OF SUBSTANCE
Profiles of Asian Women in the UK
PUSHPINDER CHOWDHRY
'Women of Substance' chronicles the achievements of over 200 Asian women in the UK from the Indian, Pakistani, Sri Lankan, Bangladeshi and East African communities - many of whom have forged a common identity since settling in Britain.
The book highlights the achievements of Asian women in such diverse fields as politics, business, the media, arts and academia. The women profiled are role models for their peer groups and the younger generation.
With an introduction by Harriet Harman MP, Minister for Women.
Paperback ISBN 1-870518-56-X £10.95

THE OTHER MIDDLE PASSAGE
Journal of a Voyage from Calcutta to Trinidad, 1858
INTRODUCED BY RON RAMDIN
Reproducing, in facsimile, the Journal of the Captain of the 'Salsette', a ship carrying Indian indentured labourers from India to the West Indies.
Paperback ISBN 1-870518-28-4 £3.95

A NEW SYSTEM OF SLAVERY
The Export of Indian Labour Overseas 1830-1920
HUGH TINKER
The first comprehensive historical survey of a hitherto neglected and only partially known migration- the export of Indians to supply the labour needed on colonial plantations worldwide, following the legal ending of slavery.
Paperback ISBN 1-870518-18-7 £11.99

BENEVOLENT NEUTRALITY
Indian Government Policy and Labour Migration to British Guiana 1854-1884
DR BASDEO MANGRU
A detailed scholarly essay on Indian migration, which, for the first time, studies the Indian background of the indentured labourers.
Hardback ISBN 1-870518-10-1 £12.95

FORTHCOMING

UGANDA: Africa's Secret Paradise
Commissioned by Yoweri K Museveni, President of the Republic of Uganda, this pioneering study and guide to the culture, environmental and scenic treasures, history and economy of one of Africa's most stable and secure nations. With a huge, relatively untapped industrial and investment potential, this book is indispensable for businesspersons, investors, diplomats and students of contemporary African history. With 320 full colour pages and a lucid text with a wealth of fascinating and practical information, this inspirational and informative work admirably captures the natural splendours of an ancient civilization, as well as its relentless and brave drive to modernization. Publication date September 1997
Hardback ISBN 1-8700518-66-7 £25

TO ORDER
All titles available by mail order enclosing payment by Cheque, PO or Visa/Access credit card payable to 'Readers Book Club'. Please add £1.50 p&p per book (UK), £3 p&p per book overseas. UK orders over £30 are post free. Send to: Readers Book Club (Books Direct), PO Box 257, Welwyn, Herts AL6 9DH.
Enquiries: Tel 0171-281 1191, Fax 0171-263 9656